Around the World in Eighteen Years

Elizabeth Welsh

ISBN 0-7414-6703-8

Printed in the United States of America

Published August 2011

INFINITY PUBLISHING
1094 New DeHaven Street, Suite 100
West Conshohocken, PA 19428-2713
Toll-free (877) BUY BOOK
Local Phone (610) 941-9999
Fax (610) 941-9959
Info@buybooksontheweb.com
www.buybooksontheweb.com

This book is dedicated to:

Will Stoner

Sam Stoner

Erin Stoner

Ben Stoner

Adam Stoner

"Promise me you'll always RemeMbEr you're bRaveER than you bELiEve, and stRongER than you sEEm, aNd smaRter than you THInk."

ChrIStopheR RobIN to Pooh

PROLOGUE

"Earthwatch is one of the world's leading environmental organizations. We use a unique model of citizen science, matching volunteers with researchers to investigate some of the greatest environmental challenges facing our planet. Earthwatch is dedicated to creating an environmental legacy through scientific research projects, education, and learning opportunities, and engaging people in field research.

Our research programs involves a global community of researchers, conservation volunteers, NGO's and businesses working together towards a sustainable environment. Earthwatch invests millions, annually, to support over 100 research projects in over 50 countries. Since 1971, Earthwatch has inspired 90,000 volunteers to join with vital conservation research projects in the field, hoping to make us not only the largest environmental volunteer, non-profit organization in the world, but also the best in the world."

— *Excerpt from Earthwatch's website, www.earthwatch.org.*

The grants cover a variety of subjects—archeology, paleontology, marine sciences, animal conservation, ornithology, botany—the list is staggering. There are jobs waiting to be done, all around the world.

This is where Earthwatch steps in. Earthwatch is able to offer the financial aid and provide scientists with volunteers to help with the work involved. Each volunteer for a specific project pays a fee. This fee covers not only his/her contribution to fund the project, but also his/her room and board at the site and a small administrative fee for Earthwatch to make arrangements and reservations.

When volunteers are accepted, they are sent an extensive history of the project and the future work that is planned for the two weeks. It states the date and time one is expected at the "staging area" where Earthwatchers meet and learn the details of their new role in science.

The briefing catalogue specifys clothing recommendations, immunization requirements, temperature, climate, and even describes the diffferent levels of activity required to best handle and enjoy the work.

For many volunteers, this may be their first travel experience alone but this should not be a reason not to join the group. Many single people go on these trips and there are often several married couples. There are best friends who join up and there are always new friends to be met, and long lasting friendships to be made.

ACKNOWLEDGEMENTS

When I sat down to write this book, I thought of a recent phrase, "It takes a village" and the good intentions it proposes. However, I also thought, oh no, not for me. I'll be able to do this by myself. What could be so hard just sitting at the computer and writing, writing, writing. WRONG!

It soon became obvious to me that although I might not need "a village", I surely did need some other people to help me. I asked several neighbors to read a chapter or two, and come back to me with words of advice, punctuation, grammar, spelling and most of all, did they enjoy the reading. And so, Rosemary, Gloria and Nikki became my advisors, critics, and proof-readers.

Then there was the computer—a machine I trusted completely until it began to misunderstand what I was trying to do or didn't like the way I was doing it and tried to wean me away from my bad habits. Before I threw the computer out the window, followed closely by myself, I realized I needed a computer guru. And so, into my life came Al and then Sandy and I was saved.

Next, I called upon an old advertising friend to help with a different choice of words and titles where needed, and Chuck came along to help.

When I needed an agent and publisher, Wendy and Michelle held out their hands to get me through the final business.

The work is finished and I hope Andrew, who was my inspiration, will be pleased with my efforts.

It has been a busy road we all traveled, and without all the people (and a few more) listed above, and all the "potholes" we DID NOT fall into, I owe them so much.

God bless and thank you for being there for me.

Liz Welsh

Table of Contents

CHAPTER 1

1984: FRANCE (MARSEILLES)
HERONS OF THE RHONE VALLEY

INTRODUCTION

In the wetlands, behind Marseilles, is the Camargue. The French government has recently begun to infringe on this area, and as a result, scientists, students, and local residents have rallied together to present their concerns. One of the results is that biologists have started to pursue studies of the breeding population of the herons and egrets who depend on these wetlands for food, especially since the Camargue is one of their stops on the flyway between Europe and Africa, when they are migrating. There are many species of birds that are constants here and many animals, including wild, white horses and bulls. The bulls, usually caught by the gauchos, are to be used in the ancient Roman arena in Arles. Pink flamingoes also stay here and provide gorgeous color to the scene.

And so we have come here to help discover what food draws the herons and the egrets to this wetland. If it happens that this land is diminished in its food supply, what could we do to provide the same menu for these birds in another location?

Here comes Earthwatch to help solve the problem!

TUESDAY, JULY 3

Right now, I am on a plane to London from Philadelphia, where I live. This is my first Earthwatch trip and I am nervous and filled with anxiety. I have signed up to be part of a team to work in the Camargue, which is a huge wetland behind Marseilles, in the South of France. I have alternate feelings of excitement, and at the same time, wondering if I should just go home. At 3000 feet in the air, the latter is not an option.

We land at Heathrow at 8 a.m. and since my plane to Marseilles is not until much later, I take a "dayroom" at the airport hotel. There I rest, shower, read, watch TV and then return to the terminal, refreshed and ready for France.

Earthwatchers have a distinct look about them when they travel. I am to learn that we usually wear t-shirts and/ or sweaters, jeans or sweat suits, hiking boots or sandals, and hats of various shapes and sizes. On the plane, I play a game with the other passengers whom I can see from my seat, and decide no one is on my list. So I have a snack, read awhile, nap, and get ready to land.

WEDNESDAY, JULY 4

We are to look for a young man holding a sign aloft, which reads "Earthwatch" and gather around him. It takes a minute for all of us to assemble and listen to his directions about luggage, customs, and where the van is parked. (I was 180 degrees wrong about what my fellow passengers were wearing; there were some Earthwatchers on my flight). We toss our luggage into the back, climb in, and head out of the city toward Tour de Valet— the name of the house and surroundings where we will live for the next two weeks.

Tour de Valet is actually a scientific Biological Station in Provence, and sits on the edge of the Camargue. The property has a large stone farmhouse, a barn and a separate building which is a dormitory for visiting students (that's us) and workers. It has a charming collection of flower and vegetable gardens, ponds, and a lovely view of trees and shrubs and the wetlands beyond,

We go to dinner in a nearby village and sit at a long table together, like the family that we will become over time. We have lots of time to talk and learn about each other. By the end of the meal we are beginning to relax and enjoy ourselves.

THURSDAY, JULY 5

Up at 7 a.m. and after a hurried breakfast, we're off in the Land Rover to see the sights, and also the "sites" where we will be working. The Camargue is a vast area of desert-like scenery combined with marshes and ponds, and a huge concentration of birds, and frogs, and rabbits, and diversified plant life. The place is also the home of large black bulls, which the cowboys (called gauchos) try to catch with their riatas. In the saline ponds are flocks of pink flamingoes that stop here every year to fill up on food as they fly south. Of course the local herring gulls torment these flamingoes by standing by the mother's nest until she rises to defend herself, and then they steal her eggs and fly off with their treasure.

We return to the farmhouse for a special luncheon by the owner of the property. It is all lovely until I am told we are eating rabbit, and it is local. Eek! There is not a palm available for me to get rid of my mouthful of what I have been seeing all morning out on the Camargue. I swallow, and find it is not so bad, after all. Small victory for me, bad news for the rabbits.

There is always a break after lunch—a lovely habit that I find admirable and could get used to very quickly. Later, we go over to Ligagneaw near Arles, to see the wondrous assemblage of eagles, rollers, skylarks, and more herons. Then over to Arles, a charming little town with cobbled streets, fields of sunflowers immortalized by Van Gogh, tiny shops and cafes and in the center of town, the bull fighting arena.

Shopping at the supermarket turned out to be a slow and careful operation since the labels were in French. Peeled tomatoes, diced tomatoes, pureed tomatoes, tomato sauce or tomato paste. (Ah, to have paid better attention in French class). Our purchases are for us to use in making our Team dinner each night in the kitchen we have. We will take turns being the cooks.

FRIDAY, JULY 6

This is the first day of our real work. We waken early, due mostly to the big fat rooster who lives at the back of the barn and enjoys crowing. We are all in the car and are led out onto the Camargue, where we are let off, one at a time in a specific area, where one will now begin to take notes on the feeding habits and the food itself, which our herons and egrets catch and immediately swallow. I am let out at a "blind" already constructed— up a few steps onto a platform with two chairs, a shelf to hold my notebook, binoculars, and over all a roof, so I don't die of sunstroke. The routine is amusing for a while. Then one could nod off to sleep. You watch a heron take slow delicate steps (with his big feet) and his head down, with his beak already half open, as he nears the fish he has spotted just below the surface of the pond. So, it's step, step, step, then peck, peck, peck, and then he lunges!!!. Three endings: 1- success; 2- a miss; 3- who knows. The fish are tiny, and herons don't smack their lips when they eat something tasty.

SATURDAY, JULY 7

Today the wind picks up and it is chilly. This is the "mistral" and is common in this part of the world. I find it spooky to be here in my spot, alone on the Camargue, and in between my notations. I await the bulls, and now, they are joined by big white wild horses, running wild, close to where I am sitting. Fortunately, I am soon joined by two other team members who are discouraged because their birds are not doing anything but just "standing around". (We all know people like that). Soon we are picked up and driven back to the station. We decide to go for dinner in a neighboring town— Salin de Giraud. It is a little country restaurant with brown checked cloths and lots of pewter ware. We have steak with Roquefort dressing. Best of the best. It is a long and lovely evening, and we stay out late— dubious choice when the alarm rings so early in the morning.

SUNDAY, JULY 8

We are up early (told ya so!) because we are going "sampling". In the U.S., this is usually a social event connected to wine, but here it turns out to be quite different. We are finding out what the herons and egrets like to eat at this particular spot in the world. This involves standing in the water and muck of a marsh pool or pond, scooping down in the water with a large flat sieve, and bringing up to the surface whatever we have caught. With tweezers, one of us picks out creature after creature, puts each one in a jar, secures it tightly, and then the specimen is taken back to our lab at the station to be identified and photographed, and then put in our notebooks. To us, most of these "creatures are unattractive and ugly" but we are not to judge!

MONDAY, JULY 9

Once again we are off to sample. This time I am on a team with three other women.

We are having a fine time laughing, making snide remarks, when Jennifer (a senior at Princeton) pulls up the sieve and in it is a HUGE leech, which stretches out to a long, long length. She screams and drops the sieve (and the leech)! I scream and drop the tweezers and the jar. The other two ladies just scream. Heinz, our Swiss scientist comes running to our aid, only to see four dumb women shaking with fear and loathing. Heinz is not amused. But there is a twinkle in his eyes. He transfers us immediately to one of the blinds to check the herons and the egrets (who wonder what those crazy noises were all about, I am sure) and substitutes a group of males, to continue the "dangerous" work. When we return at the end of our work, a picture is taken of the brave women in their jeans, hip waders, filthy shirts, preppy tennis hats, and long rubber gloves. To my knowledge, these pictures never resulted in blackmail, but we're waiting.

TUESDAY, JULY 10

And so it continues one day after another. The Earthwatch team usually has two days off, one for each week of work. On our first free day, we all pile into the Land Rover and go to Les Sts. Maries de la Mer, which I thought looks like a poor-man's Riviera. We get into our bathing suits and walk onto the nice wide beach. For the first time in my life, I am overdressed at the beach. If you are wearing a top with your two-piece bathing suit, you stand out! If you are wearing a one-piece suit, you look like an idiot. If you have no suit on at all, you are one in the crowd. Whew! None of us know where to look or where not to look. The only thing to do is to get into the Mediterranean and stay there. The water is blue, clean, and refreshing and we stay for more than an hour. When we come ashore, we race through the sand, strewn with bodies, to the bathhouse, change our clothes and pile back into the Land Rover. We drive around the streets of the resort, look at the Provence fabrics, which are "to die for", eat at a cafeteria-self-service, and then back into our car for the next sight.

Aigues Mortes is a walled city. First we check out the shops, and then check out a restaurant (why are we always hungry?)— all of which sit charmingly around a square in the center of the town. Then we walk around the city "on high". There are many walled towns and villages in France, but few of us have ever walked on top of the walls. Obviously, we take lots of photographs for it was too spectacular a view to ignore. Then back to the car, and on to Tour de Valet, thankful for such an interesting trip.

WEDNESDAY, JULY 11

When we are up and fed, we are confused because no schedule has been posted. I finally am assigned to do measuring in the lab. This is fun albeit a bit bizarre, but it is cool and quiet here and I welcome the change. Lunch is nice, then our little siesta, and then four of us go over to the rookery to see where our birds live and their nests. The babies are very cute balls of fluff. The rookery smells awful, as expected. When the windbreak gets built next year, the air will be much better. No mistral in there. We must be back by 5 p.m. because we are invited to a farmhouse, somewhere in the field of sunflowers, to meet one of the benefactors of the project. Our host treats us to wonderful olives. Then we go back to our own house and the cooks have cooked special paella for us. The students are also having a party in our dorm, so there is a lot going on tonight. Obviously, we won't get much sleep. And that rotten rooster will start up at 5:30 a.m. I wonder if I am strong enough to wring his neck!

FRIDAY, JULY 13

Up at 6:30 a.m. to do my last sampling duty. Someone has absconded with the tea kettle in our shared kitchen with the students, so there is no coffee for breakfast. This does not bode well for the rest of us and the rest of the day. But our scientist Heinz arrives and gets us coffee elsewhere, then takes us to meet a friend of his who has a big pond on his property. Now, we can really wade into the water, but all we catch in our sieve is one large fish and a few little ones. We have such a good time with the men "throwing" the sieve and then "straining" it. The ladies just stand around and laugh. Our jars are full by 10:30 a.m. so we go away, happy. Heinz drives us around to several other spots to consider but we are more interested in watching the horsemen who are chasing a herd of the bulls. We are told that this is very delicate work, takes much training, and we are not to disturb them. They may be catching bulls for tomorrow's arena's sports. We go away quietly.

Back to the station and the rest of the day we spend in the lab.

SATURDAY, JULY 14

It is Bastille Day and the country celebrates. We do also by taking our second day off. The first place we head for is Arles to see the festivities. We park across the bridge from town because there is such a crowd. We watch a parade through the cobbled streets, to the War Memorial, then listen to a few speeches. We stop to look into the Arena but no bulls, no show. We wander around and have a hamburger. Whee! That tasted good. Back to the Land Rover and off to Les Baux. This town looks really formidable; built on top of great rocks of bauxite. There is a steep road up to the town with such sharp curves that buses cannot drive up, so everyone has to walk. At the top, the view is sensational. Beautiful mountains, the Alpines act as a backdrop, and there is this bustling town, and at the far end are lovely old Roman ruins.

The ruler of this old town used to throw his enemies over the wall and watch them roll down to their deaths. (No football games that day?)

When we have seen it all, we walk back down the hill, and Heinz insists that we go to see the famous restaurant in the valley. On the way, we stop to see a wine shop in a cave, by the side of the road. We walk in and it is cool and dank. There is an electric organ and a tray of sample wines. We accept a taste or two.

Then over to Beau Maniere. I had read about this five-star gastronomic paradise in Gourmet magazine once, and here I was. Fortunately the place is not open, which is just as well, since our raggle-taggle group would not have been invited inside—that's for sure. And none of us could have afforded the $100 per serving from their kitchen. Instead, we have dinner at a charming inn in Fontvllle, go back via Arles to see the holiday fireworks. Then slowly wind our way to Tour de Valet. Tomorrow we will work.

SUNDAY, JULY 15

Up as usual at our early hour and breakfast is beginning to be a survival maneuver. I am eating stuff I would never eat at home. Almost the flies. This is because we have not been to the grocery for a few days, and also, everyone has lost track of which food belongs to which group and everyone has just grabbed whatever is there.

Off to the lab by 8 a.m. to do measuring for the whole day. I don't know if my eyes will stand much more of this tiny-tiny work. We work, eat, rest, work until 5 p.m. and then go back to our room to change clothes to go to Mr. Duggan's house for cocktails. His house is called Petit Badon, the meaning of which I am too embarrassed to ask. We go out through a French door/window, onto a roof, to have our drinks. That is a switch. There are three nice dogs already out there, so I guess this is a common occurrence at Petit Badon. After a while, we leave for a dinner at Andre Hoffman's house which is in an old tavern, renovated in the past few years to look like the typical Provencal of olden days— stone floors, rooms that go up a step or down a step, filled with comfortable couches, a kitchen with everything in stainless steel, including the counters (this is not old French Provencal!) and a also a brand new laser beam stereo. I am impressed and ask the host if he will play for us a Mozart's Piano

Concerto. One would have, thought we were in Carnegie Hall it was so beautiful.

On the way back to the Station that night, we learn that we are the first Earthwatchers to be invited to this grand house. I'm delighted we are the first and hope we aren't the last. We could easily get into this way of life.

MONDAY, JULY 16

This day is much more relaxed because, by now, a great deal of the work has been done. All that sampling and lab work, with descriptions, measuring and labeling all of those creatures from the marshes, and side trips to see or do a few necessary errands, are coming to a close. I get out of lab work today so I can sit outside our sleeping quarters, on the steps, mending the nets for more sampling for the next team to use. It is really a lovely place; this lovely old stone farmhouse, amidst miles and miles of sunflowered fields, and also bright yellow mustard flowers, and the forever-bright blue skies. No wonder painters and other artists love to come here and settle down. The air is sweet and the birds sing in the orchards all day long. Tough life! The other students studying here are from all over the world. A delightful young man from Sri Lanka is working on his doctorate, which is about dragonflies. At least that's what I call them— those winged creatures that buzz around ponds and streams and eat gnats or whatever, as they fly. One morning, this guy comes into the kitchen while our team is eating breakfast and is totally ecstatic about what is in a little box in his hand. He opens it and shows us the FIRST RED-DRAGON fly he has ever caught. We have to gape at his treasure, but end up thinking he really has caught a treasure. It is gorgeous!

Our scientists are very nice guys and never get mad at the stupid things we do. They love taking us into the nearest village— Samboc— and sitting around telling us stories of their adventures. Heinz, from Switzerland, tells us a tale of transporting 20 guillemot (a seabird) eggs over 1000 miles to new nests in Norway. (I forget what organization he was with). They wrapped the eggs in 20 heavy military socks and nestled the socks among hot water bottles. They travelled by boat and then helicopter. At one of the stops, midway through their journey, while sitting in a restaurant, they decided to refill the hot water bags. To do so, they had to leave the 20 eggs sitting on their table. As they put the eggs back in their nest with the bottles, they realized that one of the eggs no longer had a heartbeat. Ever have a guillemot pancake? According to Heinz, it is quite good. When they got to the cliffs, where they were to put the eggs on shelves that jut out from the cliffs, they were continuously growled at, day after day, by the puffins that already inhabited these cliffs. They got the eggs (minus one) to the place they were supposed to go, and later heard from Norwegian friends that all eggs hatched and grew to be big birds like their parents. I wonder if they wear those military socks, or maybe they outgrew them.

Near the end of our stay, we go over to the rookery where the egrets/herons nest and have their babies. The next team will build a windbreak for the area because some birds are lost and babies fall out of nests when that crazy mistral blows. There is a tower there that everyone climbs (except me) to see the Camargue all around us. When we return to home base, we hear that we all have been invited to dinner at an old ruined farmhouse, recently restored by a very rich family in the pharmaceutical business back in the U.S.A. We have a lovely time— eating lovely food and seeing gardens and meeting lovely people. We decide we could be happy living here.

Our last night at Tour de Valet, we are treated to dinner at La Grand Mar, nearby, at the crossroads of two country lanes, and a real atmosphere of the French countryside. A good meal with several excellent wines.

TUESDAY, JULY 17

Our last day! Of course we wake up early and aren't able to go back to sleep. But we're up, finish packing, have another survival breakfast, take more pictures to run out the film in our cameras. We leave at 10 a.m. for the drive to Marseilles airport and most of us fall asleep on the trip. We are tired. At the airport, we sit down to our last meal together. Then we board our planes for our trip back to Paris or London, then on to overnight and morning flights back to the U.S.

Provence— the land of sunflowers.

"Scoping" the Camargue.

At work in the lab.

At work in the marshes (muck).

Haute couture is it not! Ready for work.

End of the day in the marsh.

Old and charming in Arles.

Aigues Morts—a nearby walled city.

Will our LandRover make it to the town of Les Baux?

Le Baux is quite a sight.

CHAPTER 2

1985: ISLE OF JERSEY
ISLAND MARRIAGE

INTRODUCTION

Jersey is the largest of the Channel Islands, 10 miles long and 6 miles wide. The capital is St. Helier. Total population is 75,000. There are 12 parishes, each has its own coat of arms. The largest industry is banking and it rivals Zurich as a financial center. The tax system is a flat 20% on income, and there is no sales tax, capital gains tax, or estate tax. The island governs itself, levies its own taxes and issues its own currencies and postage stamps. The cows are black and white (Guernsey's cows are light brown and white).

The island is independent of the United Kingdom except in defense and foreign policy. The Queen of England is called the Duke of Normandy because the Channel Islands were part of the Duchy of Normandy when William, Duke of Normandy, conquered England in 1066. They have always remained loyal to their Duke. They are now possessions of the English Crown.

During World War Two, these islands were the only part of England occupied by the Germans, but the islanders went on with their own lives for five years. There are many great stories about the occupation, both good and bad. The Jerseyites liked the Germans better than they liked the Guernseyites. So I am told?

Karen Gottlieb is our P.I. for the Earthwatch project called "Island Marriage". She is a professor of Anthropology and Genetics at Pennsylvania State University. And we have all been accepted as Team 7 Volunteers. Karen's interest is in the population structure of the Channel Islands of all varieties– biological, geographical, social and cultural, that shape the destiny of a population and contribute to the distribution of genetic variability within the population. The project is the role that marriage plays as a micro evolutionary in these islands, especially on the island of Jersey. She hopes to expand the database to all the Channel Island's marriage patterns.

For this Earthwatch trip, I am accompanied by a friend who has never been to Europe. We decide to fly to London (the only way we can get to the Island of Jersey) five days early in order to "do" the city and all its wonderful sights.

WEDNESDAY, JULY 3

Five days later we took the airbus to Heathrow and boarded the plane to St. Helier, the capital of Jersey. Upon landing, we do our VAT-TAX thing, which will save us 10 pounds when we leave the island, check our return flights, and meet up with two EW assistants who have come to take us to our hotel in the parish of St. Quen. This is across the island and the name of the hotel is St. Etaqueral. We are in the northwest corner of the island. We are welcomed, go upstairs to unpack, change clothes, and reappear in the dining room for dinner. Everyone on the team has now arrived, and we have the usual introductory conversations.

THURSDAY, JULY 4

The next morning, Karen, our leader, explains what we will be doing to help in her research work. Mainly, we will be interviewing families in certain parishes, and taking down the genealogy of family. When our work is finished, she will put the data into her computer, take it back to the States and complete her thesis. She takes all of us in our jitney and acquaints us with the countryside and the little villages in between. She also fills us with the history of Jersey and the other Channel Islands nearby.

In St. Helier, we stop to do some chores, such as the Laundromat, the Post Office, and the Bank. By day's end we are ready for– whatever.

FRIDAY, JULY 5

After breakfast, each of us is dropped off at a location, near the homes in which we will conduct interviews. I am left at the junction of two country lanes and wonder how I should begin. At the first house I am greeted by a large shaggy dog, who lets me pet him and gives me the courage to knock at the front door. The residents are really nice people and invite me in for tea and biscuits, which I love. Then I ask and they answer– all about their immediate family, their grandchildren, aunts, uncles, and each relative they can think of. And their church. And their neighbors. And their community. I write as fast as possible, and eventually leave (with the dog) through the front gate. (The dog stayed home). The next house had no answer when I rang. And the same response at the third. This means I will have to come back another day. I do talk to some more animals, and check out the beautiful flowers in all the yards. And then the jitney arrives, and off we go to lunch.

We eat lunch, most days, across the island at St. Catherine's Bay. A lovely spot on the beach, to sit and relax. This is the only place I have seen a water fountain that has a sign on it, "Do Not Drink. This Water is Not Potable." This seems a bit weird.

We then are returned to our "locations" and work for the rest of the afternoon. Unfortunately a lot of time is often wasted in all this transporting around the island, particularly if one's interview goes on and on, or, just as bad if no one is at home and one is left sitting on a curb, or on a wall, until "pick-up" time. I ate an entire box of fresh raspberries one day ($0.55) sitting in a meadow on a rock, waiting. Could have been worse!

That evening we are taken through the garage in the backyard of our hotel, to see rooms which were built into the rock abutting the garage, and used as a German bunker, left over from the last war. Thank goodness for our guide (the hotel host) because it is sort of spooky. The rooms are still in disarray, as though the inhabitants left in a hurry. A phone and cord hung from the wall, electric wiring was still looping from walls and ceilings, and the switchboard still stood against one wall (no lights flashing). We could see out of one tiny thin window, down onto the bus stop where we will wait at a later time.

SATURDAY, JULY 6

I wake up today with the beginning, or middle of a cold, and instead of taking the trip over to Guernsey with the team, decide to stay put and in bed. I ask one of the other team members to go in my place, and one of the guys oblige. So back to sleep.

In the afternoon, I feel better, so I take the bus into St. Helier, go to the P.O. for stamps, and buy a take-out lunch and sit on a bench looking out to sea. Then buy four sweaters that I want to ship back to the States, package them up back at the P.O., and send them off. Each of the Islands hereabouts has its own sweater with its own design knitted on the front. This is similar to the Irish sweaters that are so famous, which, in case you are drowning in the ocean and you are wearing the insignia of your neighborhood or parish or town, rescuers can more easily identify you. A bit macabre but okay under certain circumstances.

The travelers return in time for dinner, as did I, and apparently they didn't see much.

Didn't read the guidebook?

SUNDAY, JULY 7

After breakfast, three of us rent a car and take off for a daytrip. First we go to the Butterfly Museum-of which I had never heard, until today. It is really a very large greenhouse, but the plants inside are all especially known to attract butterflies. These beauties go through their whole life cycle in this museum, and each stage of development has its own area open to the public. So one is able to follow the metamorphosis as it occurs, and the last area is the gorgeous butterfly. These insects live such a special life that they are free to sit on your shoulder, or on top of your head, and of course in your hand, and there is no fear of visitors.

Then on to Lawrence Durrell's famous Zoo, where the animals are used for preservation of their species, not as the usual Zoo attraction. They still have cages as a retreat, but otherwise they roam around their compounds as if they were out in the backyard playing children's games. It was the first time I had seen a Tamarind golden- and they are totally enchanting. So we take a tour of the workings of this museum, eat lunch in the cafeteria, and drive down into St. Helier and park near Elizabeth Castle. I try to convince my friends that this is where I had grown up and my family still live therein. Harumph! There is a procession that day, out to the Castle to lay a wreath at the grave of St. Helier, and everyone is very solemn and quiet. We did not go inside the Castle. It is quite a walk back and forth from the shore out there and we are glad the tide has not turned and made us run all the way.

MONDAY, JULY 8

We start back on our interviews today and I spend the morning with two new families– one of whom is generous with their life history, and the other couple act as though they want me to go away. When one is sitting in the parlor with one or two members of the family, it is fun to notice how the house is furnished, and what appliances they have, and do not have, like ours. Colors are much more subdued, lots of doilies under the lamps and antimacassars over the arms of the chairs. The ladies still wear "house dresses" and the men still wear leather shoes and shirts with ties.

I wonder how the younger generations have changed– if at all. These Channel Islands give you a feeling that they are in a different time warp than we are. And yet they can be charming and loving (they have lots of cats and dogs) and just good people. I learn much from most of them. At the end of the day, I buy a box of raspberries from a little stand at one house, and go across the road to sit in their meadow and eat the whole boxful. Yum. After dinner, we have a lecture and a slide show about the Island which is interesting.

TUESDAY, JULY 9

Another day of interviewing, sitting in meadows eating local fruit, waiting for the hourly pick-up by the team car, and wondering if this would eventually bore me, living here midst such quiet and beauty, as opposed to the hustle and bustle of the city near where I live in the States. Maybe I could have each one; 6 months of the first, then 6 months of the second. I will have to put this on my list of things to think about when I go home! Tomorrow we go over to Sark. Karen gives us a lecture and a slide show of this tiny island across the bay.

WEDNESDAY, JULY 10

Today is one of our days off and we are to take the hydrofoil to the island of Sark. Sark is the only fiefdom left, in the world. The ruler of Sark is called the Lord of Sark– in this case the ruler is a woman. As ruler, she does not have serfs (or slaves or vassals). There are many other dos and don'ts you must obey if you live on this tiny island.

You may not own pigeons because they eat the crops; no cars, only tractors and horse carts; you cannot get a divorce because that would upset the bookkeeping of the families on the island. There was once a lengthy discussion (four hours) at the Chief Pleas meeting when the people wanted one of their streets made "one way." The outcome was that eventually horses were allowed to go only one way and tractors were only allowed to go the other way. I guess that counts as "one way!"

Our hydrofoil stops off shore at the dock in Sark, because the harbor is too small for us. A tender comes out and takes us over to the island, and once on shore, we are presented with a very high hill. Which, I among others, do not intend to climb. One can rent a horse, or you can get on a tractor with a wagon attached and be taken up. At the top, there are horse-drawn carriages that will give you a tour. Islanders ride horses or bicycles or walk. There are 500 tractors registered on the island, and the island measures 1350 acres. A fast disappearing French patois is spoken, harkening back to when Sark belonged to France. There is a short shaky bridge across a chasm leading to Little Sark. The bridge is high and sways so much, I am afraid to step on it. There is a little mining operation over there, and of course more farming. Back in town I buy postcards so they can be mailed from Sark when the mail boat from Jersey comes twice a week. There is a lovely church in the center of town that has gros pointe on the pew cushions! There is a cattle show today and after the judging of the "best" there is a milking contest. The ladies in the audience are wearing their bonnets, which look like our Amish bonnets, but with longer backs and three bows.

As we get back to the hill and the boat, there is a sign in front of one of the houses reading, "Charlotte had 10 piglets this morning, and is doing fine." Try finding that kind of news in "The New York Times."

THURSDAY/ FRIDAY, JULY 11,12

We work for five or six days then have a day off. Actually, interviewing new people each day is very relaxing and one really gets caught up in their lives. I find, for example, that few people marry persons outside their own parishes. This seems very confining, because the parishes aren't that big. Also, most people do not go off the island, not even to their nearest neighboring island, Guernsey. Incidentally, the Jerseyites did not have a bad time during the war, with their uninvited German guests, except that the food ran out sometimes. Twice I am told they preferred to have the Germans with them rather than the Guernseyites. They really dislike the Guernsey folk. And yet they play them in high school athletic games each year. So there!

SATURDAY, JULY 13

This is another free day and I decide to take the hydrofoil to St. Malo, over in Brittany, France. None of the other members of our team want to go with me to see famous Mont San Michel, so I rent a red Citron for myself, and drive alone to find this special place. I immediately get lost trying to get out of St. Malo, but finally am on the correct road, wandering through lovely farmlands and meadows, cows and produce stands all there, and large ropes of garlic strung from poles. Normandy is so beautiful! The traffic picks up and I know I must be getting close to my destination. There it is! And the tide is out, meaning I can park on the sand flats that are now dry enough to hold cars and buses. I am dumbstruck at the huge church atop the piles of rocks, with water all around and flags flying, and gulls careening around the turrets of this monastery.

Lots of sightseers' restaurants and shops, on the path leading up to the monastery. We are all buying water, and more water, because it is so hot. One is allowed to walk up to the first level of the Abbey, but the heat drives most of us to go no further. We sit and people-watch.

All of a sudden, there is a blast from the siren hidden somewhere, and we all are alerted that the tide has turned and will rush in over the parking lot sooner than later. Everybody heads for the path to get their bus or car. I have long legs, so put them to work, and arrive quickly at my little red Citroen. I am out of there before the road gets squashed with traffic. I go back to St Malo, leave the car at the rental office on the pier and take a walk on the high wall around the town. There are men playing bocce on a field below me. The houses all have orange roofs, and every window box in town is filled with glorious flowers. Such a pretty sight. Then back onto the boat and back to Jersey, where at the hotel, I drink at least a dozen glasses of water. It was an exciting trip; too bad it is so hot.

SUNDAY/ MONDAY, JULY 14/15

We now switch our interviewing to two other parishes, which were not quite finished by the last team. So we do St. Martins– where we sit and wait for our pick-up ride in the graveyard of the village church and gossip and eat local tomatoes and strawberries– and then to St. Lawrence, in the pouring rain, and find ourselves not particularly welcome, in our Wellies and raincoats, but we do get enough information to fill out our forms.

Our driver takes us to a small hotel in town to reward our determination, and then gives us the rest of the day to do "whatever." We go to the Museum to see the Matisse exhibition, then through the market to stare at the goods, and then to the German Museum which houses pictures and mementos of the days of the Occupation.

TUESDAY, JULY 16

This is our last day and we fly around, packing our belongings, returning stuff to its rightful owners, and places around the hotel. I grab someone who is driving into St. Helier. He gives me a ride so I can go to the hardware store and buy the seeds of the flowers I want to try to grow back in the States. (P.S. They did not flourish!)

WEDNESDAY, JULY 17

Off to the airport and amidst hugs and a few tears, we all get on board the plane back to London and onward to our home bases.

INSERT

To prepare us for our interviewing, we are given a copy of the research form, which we will fill out as we make our calls. During the interview the head of the household or his wife will be asked questions, regarding their marital status, birthplace of the spouse, birthplaces and surnames of his/her parents, grandparents and siblings, and of his/her spouses' parents, grandparents and siblings if they lived on the Channel Islands. A short genealogy will be taken and the marital couple will be asked if they share any relatives in common which is a non-offensive way to inquire about inbreeding. This is not unusual for island communities. There are few marriages between the islands and this lack of human mating resembles the laws they have about their dairy cattle– to keep the breed pure a Guernsey or Jersey cow which leaves its respective island, is not allowed to return. Therefore, one could postulate that the genetic result would be homogeneity within the island and perhaps within the parish, and heterogeneity between islands and maybe between parishes. Ergo, our work for the next two weeks is to try to get some answers.

INSERT

One afternoon, driving back from our interviews, as we came along the beach road, the tide is out, and like Mt. San Michel, people were hurrying along the cement path toward Elizabeth Castle. All the boats in the harbor had their "props" out to keep them upright while the tide was out, so we loved that particular scene. Elizabeth Castle looms high against the sea beyond and has always been a fortress to protect the island. One time, when the French approached and handed a document to the commanding officer at the Castle, telling him that the French were taking over, the officer looked at the paper, appeared to read it, and then returned it to the Frenchman simply saying, "I don't read French." End of situation.

INSERT

The Guernsey people generally do not get along well with the Jerseyites, and refer to them as "Toads". This name has reason to it, since Jersey is known for an abundance of these large and small amphibians.

In turn, the Jersey people refer to their island neighbors as "Donkeys". No reason given and no one told me why.

INSERT

One great sight on Jersey is the changing of tides. The tides here are the second largest changes in the world, the first being on the Bay of Fundy, in Canada. To the side of St. Helier, where the shops begin to fade out, and you are driving down the shore road, you notice that if the tide is out (and it really, really goes OUT), all the boats, both big and small, have wooden planks, set at an angle from the bottom of the bay and slanted upward against the side of the boat. This way, when there is no water in which to float, the boat has supports on both sides to keep it upright; when the tides come in the planks are fixed to work like oars, and just rise with the water, and can eventually be pulled into the boat when it sets sail. Their tides have been known to rise and fall to as much as 10 feet!

INSERT

Another interesting sight on Jersey is the appearance of an animal that I have only had acquaintance with in childhood books– a Hedgehog. Remember Mrs. Tiggywinkle, from Beatrice Potter. See them all over the country lanes here.

RESEARCH FORM:

QUESTIONNAIRE FOR INTERVIEWS

Questions should be asked of informant regarding himself/herself and (1) siblings (2) father and mother (3) paternal and maternal grandparents (4) spouse (5) spouse's siblings (6) spouse's father and mother and (7) spouse's paternal and maternal grandparents.

Name

Address

Occupation

Birthplace

Birthdate

Where did you live during your childhood?

Marital status

Where were you living when you met your spouse?

Where was your spouse living?

How old were you when you met your spouse?

How old was your spouse when you met?

Where were you living at the time of marriage?

Where was your spouse living at the time of marriage?

How old were you at the time of your marriage?

How old was your spouse at the time of your marriage?

When were you married (month, day, year)?

Where were you married?

If your marriage did not take place in your parish or the parish of your spouse, why was that?

Do you and your spouse have any relatives in common (excluding your children)?

How many children have you had?

Where were they born?

When were they born?

Where do you live now?

If they don't live on Jersey, why not?

Have you ever resided outside of Jersey for any period of time? Why? When?

Did you ever date people from Guernsey?

A Jersey Cow.

A St. Helier street.

Chapter 2: Island Marriage

Backyard patio at L'Etaq.

Butterfly Museum

Zoo—Golden Tamarind

Tide's out to Castle Island St. Helier harbor.

Chapter 2: Island Marriage

Path from Elizabeth Castle back to land.

The Germans are gone! Liberation Gate.

Sight-seeing cart on Sark.

Shakey bridge from Sark over to Little Sark.

CHAPTER 3

1987: KENYA
INSIDE LAKE NAIVASHA

INTRODUCTION

Lake Naivasha is Kenya's second largest freshwater lake. It is located north of Nairobi, about a 1-1/2 hours drive through the bed of the Rift Valley. Just to its north is the other lake, Nakura, which we will see later. Naivasha plays an important part in the life of this area. It has commercial fisheries, provides irrigation for surrounding farmlands, attracts tourism, and is important for wildlife conservation.

In the past few decades, two species have been introduced to this lake; one, an animal, and two, a floating water fern called Salvinia. The latter is our study target. This plant has had devastating effects on the plant life because it forms large mats in the shallows and in papyrus lagoons and therefore, threatens the growth of lower vegetation in the lake ecosystem. We hope to map the effect and the extent of Salvinia and to propose actions to hamper its spreading and impacting on lives in the surrounding communities.

Our recommendations will be prepared for the Ministry of Tourism and Wildlife to be considered in the future management of the lake

SATURDAY/ SUNDYAY, JULY 11, 12

To write that I am excited about this trip would take pages and pages of adverbs and adjectives. I won't try but as I board the plane to London on July 10th, I am in a state of rapture.

The flight to Heathrow goes smoothly and faster than I remember and although we (and several other planes) have to circle for a while, we all look as if we are suspended by strings as we bounce around the clouds. Think we were late, we aren't. I have reserved a "day room" since my flight to Nairobi isn't until 6:30 p.m. and I have many hours to wait. At first, I think I will take a bus to Hampton Court. I find that on weekends this bus doesn't run on its regular schedule. So that is out. Finally stay at the hotel, read, shower, go to their dining room early for some supper, and am at my gate in time.

The trip to Kenya is partly over the Sahara desert and I am stunned by the fact that there are high dunes and great sweeping valleys in between, and the colors that fade in and out of all this sand is indeed breathtaking. We arrive in Nairobi early in the morning, and I go directly to the Norfolk Hotel which is renowned for its beauty, its service, its comforts and most of the travelers to Kenya–plane pilots, bush pilots, safari goers, business people, and people like me– can't wait to get there and settle in. I do the usual routine, then have breakfast, and walk to the nearby museum and then go to the Snake Park. That is a mistake for I see all the snakes that live in this area (green or black mambas, who kill in a second, cobras). I could go on but I get frightened all over again. Have lunch on the porch with a pilot from Swissair, and he introduces me to several men he knows from previous visits, and the afternoon passes pleasantly with a table full of beers in front of us. Then back to my room, another rest, dinner downstairs in their Ibis Grill, and then I buy my first souvenir of Africa, a little ostrich made of straw with what looked like a tutu round his waist.

The next morning, I oversleep and am running a half hour late to be in the lobby, to be picked up by Earthwatch. They are later than I am, so I wander around the lobby and I hear my name called. I turn and see one of the hotel boys holding up a blackboard on a stick, and there is a bell ringing, and my ride has arrived. Slightly mortified at all this publicity, I gather my luggage and myself, and go to the Land Rover with Peter, the driver, and six other Earthwatchers inside. I squeeze in and off we go to Elsamere on Lake Navasha, where we will work and live for the next two weeks.

MONDAY, JULY 13

We head out of Nairobi, on our way to Naviasha, along a road where cows, goats and sheep are tied right next to the highway. Men are asleep on hillocks near their animals, while the women walk along with huge bundles on their heads. What perfect posture they have, to keep their bundles from falling! Everyone is bare-footed.

When we come to the town of Naivasha, I am shocked at how primitive it is... and very dusty. We turn here on the road to Elsamere, which is our destination.

Elsamere is the former home of Joy Adamson, who made Elsa, her lion friend, a world known and loved animal whom she cultivated (as in friendship) and brought her to this home, to study, paint pictures of, and generally care for. When Joy died, she left this property to a scientific organization to be used for further study in any of the natural sciences, of which Earthwatch was considered one. Hence, our welcome to this most beautiful place of rolling green lawns down to Lake Naivasha, tall trees inhabited with herds of chattering Colobus monkeys, vegetable gardens at the back of the house, and even their own dairy cattle. A staff of Swahili natives see that we are fed regularly (including the cows), cook amazing meals, serve tea on the lawn at 4 pm each day, and patrol the grounds at night to keep the "Hippos" from coming up from the lake to eat our vegetable garden.

And so we arrive. The road from Naivasha to Elsamere (and I use the word "road" very loosely) was such a combination of rocks and chunks of broken cement that we were really ready for a lovely sit-down lunch. Then off to unpack and rest in the rooms to which we have been assigned. We meet again for tea, exchange info between members of the team, the staff, and we are given the list of our duties, and time periods, and what to generally expect in the next two weeks. Then, we are served a gorgeous roast beef dinner in the elegant dining room, ending with real whipped cream on our dessert. By this time, we are heavy-lidded, and go off to our rooms and pleasant dreams.

TUESDAY, JULY 14

The next morning we pile into two dirty jeeps and head for Koranga– an old house on the edge of the lake. Graduate students live here. They are also studying the gradual shrinking of this lake, mainly due to the influx of the voracious weeds that are choking the life of the lake. The lake is large and very necessary, not only for the life "in" the lake but also for life "around." We need to get rid of these plants infringing on this lifeline on all levels.

We walk through a meadow, and up to the top of hill that overlooks the lake. From here we can see exactly how far these plants, mostly salvinia, have advanced, and of course, everyone wants to speculate how long it will take to make the lake useful again.

After some serious thoughts and considerations, we go back to our jeeps and drive back. On the way, we are shown an array of wildlife... birds like crowned cranes, herons and ibis, rollers, fish eagles and mouse birds with long tails. Passing a savannah, we see fourteen giraffes, a herd of eland, some impala, and some Thompson gazelles. Who needs Hollywood when we have everything right here. Down the road a giraffe decides to get out of the way of our jeep, and gracefully steps over the high fence to safety– the fence behind which we assumed he was supposed to stay.

Back at Elsamere, at tea, we discuss the various fields of study, from which we make our choices for the coming week. I choose Botany. I will regret this, a few days later. This has been long and we are all tired so we stop talking and go to bed.

WEDNESDAY, JULY 15

The next morning we are awakened at 6:30 a.m. but stay under the covers for a few more minutes. We are beginning to feel that our work is a bit haphazard and that none of us feel guilty about the few extra minutes. The weather here is glorious– clear bright days, cool nights, no humidity, and nice hot sun. We leave in a full bus to go to Koranga again. This time we see a zebra, walking aimlessly here and there, and a dik-dik crosses in front of us on the road. We get down to the marsh again and start making grids (squares) in the weeds, in preparation to pulling out all the plants, categorizing them, listing them, so we can begin to see what grows most often and which specimens seem to be the most dense. One of us loses both her shoes in the muck when she takes a step. We find them. After lunch we all sit around trying to make some identifications of all the stuff we have found. We learn several important things that day. One is how to keep bending over– like the Kenyans do all the time, without coming up eventually with really sore backs. Two–that the whole lake is surrounded by electrified wire fences to keep the hippos from coming up into the farmer's lands at night to steal food. Then in the morning, the fences are turned off so fishermen and other people can use the lake.

All of us are also beginning to feel that our goals are a bit haphazard, and we need more definite direction. We go for a short walk before going back to the marsh, and I am alone on one of the trails when all of a sudden there appears in the middle of my path a snake. I stop. He stops. Then he raises his head that spreads out like a flower and I realize it is a small cobra. I know enough not to turn and run, but I would really like to do exactly that. It becomes a battle of who moves first. And where. I am terrified, but think he (she) is also. Finally the snake drops to the ground and slithers off. I collect what's left of my wits, casually turn around and go slowly back to the marsh.

Dinner is late that night, and we are all seated, when Dr. Harper arrives, and after introducing himself, and giving a little speech, he starts to eat. We are a bit surprised at his casual attitude, since we are bursting with questions, but nothing is said. We feel strange about this.

THURSDAY, JULY 16

This has been the longest and hardest day ever. After breakfast, we pile into the Land Rover and head directly over to Koranga again and go down to the marshes, where three of us stake out four grids. The last one is quite a ways out in the water, and this time we really get wet; standing in the water in my boots and socks for about four hours. We are potting plants and measuring and keeping notes, etc. We are also in the blazing sun. Occasionally, I think I might keel over, but that option is not very appealing. Come back up to the house at Koranga and then we hurry back to the marsh to finish our tasks. Ian (he is seventeen) and I are getting more and more uncomfortable and my boots will never be the same. We finally finish our grid work and all of us pile back into the Land Rover and drive around the whole lake– the long way– but scenic, to the town Navaisha, to get some gas in the car. We slosh out of the Land Rover and buy some post cards, but we are tired and don't buy anything else. (Our day would come!)

That night, at dinner, we have a briefing session with Dr. Harper. It is quite a muddle to all of us, and as one said afterwards, "He is not a good communicator". Amen. One tidbit from our drive back from Navaisha makes us all the more unbelieving about what we are seeing. When there is roadwork to be done, the men have no sign or flag to warn drivers that they are working there, so they throw limbs and branches all over the road, and this is their way of warning motorists.

FRIDAY, JULY 17

Today was less spectacular than yesterday, in that we repeat the work schedule, and go up the hill to eat lunch at Koranga. There have been two men hanging around the house there, and it makes all of us nervous, so we continue to hang around longer after lunch, to watch our belongings in our locked car. One from our group goes for a walk in the woods nearby and sees a great black hornbill. I see a hoopoe in the tree opposite the house– a rare-bird-kind of day.

Back to Elsamere early, for teatime, bathing, dressing, and sitting down to a sumptuous roast duck dinner, with fried bananas on ice cream for dessert.

On the ride home that day, a giraffe comes and stands in our way, so we stop and get out and talk to him. He is about thirty feet away, and we are having a lovely visit, when he simply turns and walks into the bushes. He looks completely bored with us.

SATURDAY, JULY 18

Today turns out to be an adventure. All of us leave right after breakfast to drive to the Mau Escarpment, which are the mountains where the Mau Mau, the political enemies, come from and hence hang out, when they aren't killing and destroying all around the countryside. On the road up the mountains is a great photo-opt of the fertile green valley below; some thatched roofed huts, lots of shepherds with herds of cows or flocks of sheep. On the ridge of the escarpment, there is a little boy about two years old, who already has his stick (staff) and is apparently a shepherd-in-training. The adult men have blankets wrapped around their shoulders for warmth, because at the altitude here (10,000 feet) the air is clean but often cold. The air is filled with beautiful birds and, on the way down from the mountain; we have a real-live secretary bird cross right in front of us. If you are not familiar with how they look, they have a large feather stuck behind their head, which seems to be a pencil stuck behind his ear.

In the middle of all this beauty, the Land Rover throws a back wheel. Thank goodness two of our Earthwatchers know how to fix this mess, although there are several gasps at several intervals, when the jack holding up our car, starts to tilt. We finally sit by the road and eat our lunch and then continue down the mountain without a spare tire. We are nervous because we are getting low on gas. We stop once to pick some flowers, in what looks like an Alpine meadow– filled with red-hot poker plants. There are three shepherds in the meadow– a grandfather, a father, and a grandson. Grandpa comes over to us carrying his sharp metal spear and many of us envision our mortality at this moment. But he is friendly. We want to take his picture, but are afraid to ask. Our driver speaks Swahili, but doesn't say a word. Instead, we just continue on our way. It begins to rain, and the windshield wipers don't work. The Gods are obviously sick of our troubles, and provide a safe, although at times scary, ride back to Elsamere. When we pull onto our own property, Ian gets down on his knees and kisses the ground.

Tomorrow we are to stay on our own property... a distinct relief to all of us.

SUNDAY, JULY 19

Sunday is often a "chill out" day on an Earthwatch trip. And so it is today. We rise an hour later, have a leisurely breakfast (this heavy cream we have, direct from the cow is warm and "to die for" which is what will happen to us if we keep using it). Then the whole team meets out on the lawn (with the monkeys) to listen to a talk by Dr. Harper's assistant about our project, its aims, and its long-reaching effects from what we are discovering, etc. Now we understand better why we are here. Have a coffee break and walk down to the lake and two of us come back to the house to work on our quadrant reports. Then a lovely lunch of chicken curry.

The tourists begin arriving, as it is open house on Sundays. They are polite and gracious and are impressed by our volunteering. We stay with them for a while, and then go back to our rooms and do chores and rest and by the time the visitors have left, it is time for dinner, a brief meeting about tomorrow and then off to bed.

MONDAY, JULY 20

We drive to Lake Nkuru for the shopping, the park and the lake. The Land Rover breaks down again after we pass through Naivasha, and meanwhile, we pick up a man who has also had car trouble and we are packed in like proverbial sardines in very little space. Our car is finally fixed, in Nkuru and we have to leave our new passenger in the town because his car needs more help and we must be on our way. Nkuru is quite a bustling small town with several hotels, lots of shops, and on blankets spread out on the sidewalks we find sandstone carvings and some woodcarvings. All of us are very much tourists here and buy bags, jewelry, art and whatever. Then into the Land Rover and off to the lake! Pink birds, white sand, and blue sky. Africa at its most beautiful!

However the sand is not real sand; it is a mixture and is called the soda lake. These soda flats are brilliant white and VERY dangerous, because you sink when you stand on the bank of the lake. We drive across this "soda" beach very slowly until we begin to sink. There are other cars that are sinking along with us. We all get out, and everyone is pushing or pulling or putting floor mats under the tires, and whatever it will take to return us to traction so we can back out of the mess. We are all out except one car that is badly embedded and the young Swedish occupants are getting desperate. All of a sudden, from a rim of trees by the beach, appear a half dozen young black men, who circle the car, count to three and then lift the entire car with their hands, and walk it off the beach. There are gasps, handshakes, thanks, etc. but no money is allowed. What great publicity for the townspeople here. So should the world!

We now drive around the entire lake. It is so bumpy we are reluctant to move because we decide we will break something in some part of our body. We stop at the Lion Lodge where we have cold beers and a hoard of baboons begging for just one sip. No way. The countryside here is full of animals—warthogs, water buffalos, impalas, zebras, and gazelles. We gape and gape, resulting in getting back to Elsamere late for dinner. We eat leftovers and off to bed.

TUESDAY, JULY 21

It is to be a good day, except for one little incident– not so little however, when it first happens. Three of us drive over to Koranga, pick up one more volunteer and go down the hill to the marshes to dig up some more plants. We are quite far out in the muck– beyond the fence wire– and one of the men calls over to me to bring them some bags in which to put some plants after they had washed the mud out of the roots. I cannot explain what got "into" me at that moment, but I swear I heard a voice say to me… "Don't do that!" I stop, literally, in my tracks, holding the bags, and shout back "No". At which point, the young boy Ian comes towards me and reaches for the bags. He touches the fence and then screams as he falls to the ground, having been shot through with electricity… the FENCE HAD NOT BEEN TURNED OFF THAT MORNING! He is crumpled in the water, but is still conscious. I grab my rake, with its wooden handle and stick it through the water to him, and the other guys get him and themselves over the fence. We all head back to shore in a big hurry. The Land Rover comes to pick the plants and us up and we go back to Koranga. Ian is coming out of his shock by then but we all sit around, waiting until everyone has recovered enough to make the drive back to Elsamere. Whew! I will never know what stopped me from getting that shock– and I'm sure I would have been hurt.

On the way back we meet some Masai men, herding some goats, sheep and cows. The Masai always look rather formidable to me, with their faces slightly painted, their tall, thin stature, and those long spears they carry. We stop because we can't get by them, and they see we have sodas in the back of the car. They bring out money to buy 11 sodas and some beer from us. We have been forewarned never to take a picture of Masai without their permission, but this time we have done them a favor, and so one of our men asks them if it would be okay. They nod yes, and we jump out and take their pictures quickly, jump back in the car, and speed on our way. Once we feel safe again, we congratulate ourselves on our apparent coup. Ian is attended to by a local doctor and put to bed to rest. They have saved tea for us, which we really love and go to bed early, feeling very, very lucky.

WEDNESDAY, JULY 22

Today, several people are down with a nasty little virus, and so there are no trips at this point. Which is fine with me because I have been asked to draw pictures of all our samplings. Very appealing job, since I do not have to be mucking around in the marshes. A small group of us, who are staying put today, have a wonderful lunch, which as always is a feast. Then we all go back to our quiet little chores and the day passes quickly. At dinner, the conversation turns to the disappointment which some of us are feeling because we still have three days to go and no one seems to have any plans as to what we are to do. There is a strike in Mombasa and all our new equipment from England, is sitting there on the dock and no one knows when it will be delivered to Naivasha. What a mess.

THURSDAY, JULY 23

The next day, I begin to feel sick and decide to stay at the house, which I do, and I have no idea who goes where or why or when. By evening, I feel much better and thank goodness because it's another roast beef dinner—my favorite. After dinner, we see a film about Beryl Markham and about the wild society life, here in the Rift Valley after World War I, carried on mostly in mansions which were built right here around Lake Naivasha. Wow! Those years must have been a continual party.

Realizing that something has to be done with this team of forlorn volunteers, it is decided that we will take a trip over to Hell's Gate, a large parcel of parkland, across the road, and soon to play a major part in the area, as a real refuge and scientific study area.

FRIDAY, JULY 24

Hell's Gate is not a long drive, so we are all there, have paid our money, and are in the Park by 10 a.m. We are treated to the sight of many animals and birds as we go up and down every dirt road and we have to get out of the car time and time again, because the road is so bad and the car can't get us over and around the rocks, with such a weight in the car. There are lots of gorges and monoliths throughout the rocky terrain. We find a nice plateau, so decide to sit there and have our lunch. On one ledge below us, we see, hunched against the wall, a little Rock Hyrax that lives only here, and in spite of its size, is actually a member of the elephant family. Grazing near us are a group of Cape buffalo, who are known to be fierce, and we eat our lunch in quite a hurry, in case they come nearer and we have to abandon our spot. I offer to stay with the car while the others trek down to see a spring, when suddenly another car drives up and a lady Park Ranger jumps out of the car, and demands 30 shillings for our entry into the park. She has hijacked a young Dutch couple to drive her around the park looking for us. They have driven on all the main roads while we are on the back dirt roads, and so it takes a while to find us. The poor couple had only wanted to stop in Hell's Gate for a quick look before going on to Nakuru and the rest of their tour. They are from Amsterdam and speak English, so we three sit down and have a nice chat while the ranger goes running after our driver. Eventually everyone is gathered together, the Dutch couple is excused, the lady ranger recovers her fee, and we get in the car to see a steam plant, and a Masai village. Also a lava flow.

Back at Elsamere for tea, and now I have decided to leave Elsamere on Sunday, and go to Nairobi, since I feel I am sightseeing enough here, and if this is what the next few days will be like, I'd rather be doing some sight-seeing on my own, elsewhere. After dinner that night, a neighbor gives a lecture on the flowers, wild and otherwise, which grow in this region. It is delightful and inspires all of us to learn to garden correctly.

SATURDAY, JULY 25

It is Saturday and today is a full workday. Breakfast and then off to Crescent Island to do quadrants from the lakeside up to the big papyrus which grows to the road. Two of us work fast and do 395 meters before we break for lunch. We continue our work and have a nervous hour or so, as the Cape Buffalo seem to be interested in what we are doing, watching us closely. We are not about to share information with them and when we are done, our backs and necks are all "cricked" from bending over all day. On the way home, we stop at the sarong market, run by women from the nearby village. We have been told that they expect us to bargain for prices with them. Since the top price is only $3.00, I think that is so cheap that I am not interested in bargaining. Several from my team look at me as if I am crazy, but for all the handiwork these women have put into this work, I cannot pay them less. I am scorned! But I pay– get the prettiest sarong, and strut back to the car.

SUNDAY, JULY 26

Today is the day I am planning to leave Elsamere due to a lack of any work, and so I wake up at the usual time, have another one of those wonderful breakfasts and then coffee out on the lawn, with the monkeys still chattering above us in the trees. I do a small chart for two of the assistants, without being asked to do it– probably because I am feeling guilty about leaving early.

I am all packed and ready to leave with my ride to Nairobi, when the phone rings and it is my driver who complains that "something" has come up and he is unable to drive me. I momentarily panic and wonder what the "something" is (a giraffe in his living room?) when one of the team comes to me to announce that her guests here at Elsamere will be driving back to Nairobi and will gladly take me along.

I leave soon after, and the Murrays (my car drivers) must stop to visit with a friend near Safari land, so I wait in the parking lot for them. Within seconds, I am surrounded by a flock of Vervet monkeys, who are very cute, very playful and very much a nuisance. They want to get into my purse, they sit on my shoulders and smell my hair, they are interested in everything I do and say. One comes and sits right beside me, and I do not know if it is safe to put my hand on him or not. I decide to mind my own business. I start to sing a little song, wondering how the whole group will react; they are stunned. They sit quietly and watch my face. Then they casually back away, climb up a near-by tree and sit there staring down at me.

The Murrays finally arrive, and off we go. Mr. Murray is a doctor, and he works with the Masai, teaching and healing them. I ask him if it is true that the Masai drink only blood and/or milk, which I have heard is true. They do NOT do this; the worse part of their diet is that it is over 50% plain fat! Our conversation is fine and thank goodness because it takes my mind off the children along the road who are hanging live rabbits from their extended hands in hopes of selling them to passerby. Ugh!

I arrive at the Nairobi Safari Club in Nairobi, which is clean and well appointed and where I spend the night. I miss the sounds of Lake Naivasha and the rustle and bustle of the animals there that only come out at night to see and be seen.

MONDAY, JULY 27

After a good night's sleep, I wake up in my posh surroundings, have breakfast in the room, and go down to the lobby. I have stashed most of my luggage in the lobby so retrieve it and the cab comes to take me to the airport. This is the city airport and it takes me some time to find the right hangar for the "bush" plane, but finally do and they are waiting for me. Get on the little plane and away we go, bumpily over the mountains with little Masai villages, looking like pie plates, in all the valleys. The dirt roads look terrible below us and it must take hours to drive along them. We land on a tiny airstrip where our landing is aborted because an elephant is feeding on our runway. We circle twice, and with his full stomach, the elephant has moved to the right. We come in close to him and he doesn't seem bothered a bit. A jeep picks us up and transports us to a nearby Lodge, where I wait for another pick-up from the tented camp where I have reservations. We drive about 15 km into the bush to camp. Have lunch, go to my camp/tent and unpack, and go for an afternoon "game run". We see dozens of animals and it is glorious to see their freedom. A fine scene to behold.

TUESDAY, JULY 28

The next morning, while having breakfast in the dining tent, I am told that my plane back to Nairobi has been delayed and will be late in the day. I am nervous about this schedule—mostly because I am joining the team of Earthwatchers from Elsamere for our farewell dinner in Nairobi that night. So instead, I decide to take a ride with one of the workers at the camp, who is driving to the city. Then I wonder if this is a safe thing to do. I am concerned but really stuck. It turns out that the driver is not a worker at the camp but a private driver for a Saudi Arabia couple and I have been put in their car (without their permission). For the first hour, I am terrified that they will toss me out of the car. But their attitude softens and I am allowed to stay. Phew! I am very relieved.

I am dropped off at the New Stanley Hotel, which is primarily known for the huge tree that sits in the middle of the outdoor dining area. On this tree are personal messages left from all sorts of people all over Kenya and beyond, looking for each other, looking for rides to all sorts of destination, pilots looking for passengers on not-filled flights into the bush, business cars, "Dear John" letters—someone should write a book about the stories displayed here.

The Earthwatchers all gather at the Hong Kong Restaurant, and we have a grand time reliving our experiences together the past two weeks. And then it is time for goodbyes as we are taken to the airport outside the city. We all go home on our various flights to our own part of the world. We are thrilled with our journey, and quite sad to leave all these adventures behind us.

Elsamere.

For tea and scones at 4:00 p.m.

Our lake... Lake Naivasha.

Our transportation.

Chapter 3: Inside Lake Naivasha

Headquarters at marsh.

Me and the rare bird hoopoe.

At work.

At work.

Chapter 3: Inside Lake Naivasha

Our group with the Masai.

One bright spot- the red hot poker.

A scary moment at Lake Nkuru.

Chapter 3: Inside Lake Naivasha

CHAPTER 4

1988: GIBRALTAR
ROCKS OF GIBRALTAR

INTRODUCTION

Gibraltar is a peninsula, which juts out into the Mediterranean Sea, surrounded by Spain, and is known for the gigantic rock that covers most of the area and is referred to as The Rock of Gibraltar. Today, it is separated from Spain by a "checkpoint" through which you must pass to get into Gibraltar, and an airstrip that serves both commercial and military planes for their landings. In the Treaty of Utrecht (1713), Spain surrendered Gibraltar to Great Britain who turned it into a military base. Only Spaniards and Gibraltar residents may cross into this British Dependency; any others may come by plane, or by boat from Tangier.

The name of our Earthwatch expedition is "The Rocks of Gibraltar" which is a funny name in view of the fact that "The Rock" occupies all the space available on this peninsula; and any other rock which one would see would be along the beach, or in someone's garden. Whatever. Our objective will be to record all the 18th and 10th century gravestones and a few from the 20th century to examine attitudes towards death, taking into consideration at the same time the influence of local Spaniards and come to some conclusions about how memorials affect the feeling of Colonialism in such territories. Photographs, cemetery plan and often rubbings can also help identify the colonial attitudes.

TUESDAY, MARCH 29

After taking a few days in Morocco, my friend and I arrive in Tangier to take the hydrofoil across the Mediterranean (about 10 miles) to Gibraltar. We are due there by dinnertime. Surprise! The hydrofoil is not running that day– it has been hired by a private party, to have a party on the ship all day. So we have to hang around Tangier (not so bad since we take a tour and have a nice lunch) until mid afternoon when we can board the ferry to Algeciras in Spain. We go through customs, etc. and then try to get transportation around the Bay of Gibraltar, which is not as easy as we hoped because of the animosity between the United Kingdom and Spain over the territorial rights to Gibraltar. We finally persuade a cab driver to take us. There is a "Check-point Charlie" at this border, and we have to carry our luggage a distance to the U.K. side.

We arrive at our hotel late, but find all the Earthwatchers still in the hotel restaurant, so we sit with them, have a bite to eat, and then all of us go up to bed early.

WEDNESDAY, MARCH 30

The next day, we have a few hours to settle in, and then walk over to the cemetery, which lies directly between the sheer slope of the Rock and the only airstrip on the peninsula. Harold, our professor and leader, explains how the work will be conducted, the forms which have to be filled out for each gravestone, why we are doing all this work, and what to expect at the end of the project according to the success of our endeavors. We work for a few hours, under supervision trying to make sense of our efforts. Then, we return to the hotel to cook our own dinner (we take turns, during our stay, preparing our own dinner each night for our group), ask questions and get answers, and finally go to bed, feeling ready, willing, and able (?) to start the next day.

THURSDAY, MARCH 31

We are at the cemetery by 9:00 am the next day. The Rock mesmerizes all of us, particularly because we are right below this sloping "face" and we think of avalanches, or storms, or even stray stones which could come sliding down, and we would end up covered by one of these possibilities and would never be seen again. After another day, we forget about what's above us and concentrate on what's below us. There are rules in cemeteries of which we were naïve. For example, you must never lie down on top of a gravestone (like after eating lunch and resting one's back; you must not sit on a grave stone (like to eat your lunch); you must not talk if a person comes into the cemetery to kneel, to pray, to lay flowers, etc. anywhere close to where you are working – just a few restrictions due to the somber atmosphere of this place. Not a problem. So we bend, sit on the ground, stoop, turn sidewise and even hang over the top of the stone– anyway to help read some of the inscriptions and record them. And of course we are to be VERY careful not to disturb any part of the stone because I suppose we could end being vandals. But we all behave and have a good time trying to interpret some of the writings. One we particularly loved has a dedication to the life of a sailor who had apparently fallen from a mast on his ship, due to a severe case of inebriation. The other side of the coin, so to speak, is the sadness of the deaths of three children, who had died from disease, all in one family, and all at the same time, and all buried in one grave.

So we toil and record and also begin to time the arrival of the commercial planes that land on the airstrip, taking note of who is, and who isn't on time. We can report that British Air is the winner, and therefore their pilots become our mid-morning heroes.

One of the days, there is to be an interment of another body in the old, large tomb near where we are working. The workmen have to open the crypt the day before so it will be ready for the ceremony the next morning. Of course, that leaves the mausoleum open, and of course we HAVE to go over and look down into the chamber below. I carefully go down two of the four steps and decide this is not only a very bad thing to do, but I can see the shelves around the sides of the tombs, and even a few stray bones on the dirt floor. I leave in a hurry. I am totally spooked and decide I have just crossed some serious religious line and am doomed. My group laughs heartily and I am truly abashed. One of life's bad moments.

FRIDAY, APRIL 1

We work today, but the rest of Gibraltar is off for the Easter weekend. Some of the local people arrive to straighten out and clean the gravestones and the graveyard around them.

We figure out that it takes two of us to do 40 graves per day. There is a form to be filled out for each grave, so my friend does all the measuring of size and shape and I do all the writing in the form. I also draw pictures of the stones, since many are decorated with flowers and angels, and other pictures. All the gravestones will eventually be photographed because one worker may catch a carving that the other one misses. This is a way to be more complete.

We take about 45 minutes for our lunch of cheese sandwiches and fruit, and then work again until about 4 pm. Sitting or standing that much in the sun begins to show our tan. Some of us decide to wear shorts when the days are this sunny. There are a large number of planes today because of the holidays, so we don't do much talking, as the siren is going off constantly as the planes roll in. On our walk back to the hotel, we often stop at a special ice cream shop where they have excellent ice cream.

SATURDAY, APRIL 2

At work today, we decide to have a cocktail party tonight– celebration of course while the rest of the world is also celebrating. After lunch– cheese sandwiches and fruit, again– two of us sneak across the airstrip (no sirens at this time) to buy food for the party. We try to avoid getting caught by Harold, but of course he sees us. I even hide from him behind a car at one point. Wrong! But he lets us go and we lug our stuff straight back to the hotel. The party starts at 6 pm and everyone arrives at once, including Harold. So of course, he couldn't stop us when he saw us shopping. He knew all along what was going on. We now know that the two of us would make very bad criminals. The people stay until nine. A few stay later and we cook hamburgers, but it is late and everyone goes to bed.

SUNDAY, APRIL 3 (EASTER)

Today, we are going to Seville. When we leave at 7 am, all of us are still groggy with sleep. It's a rather bumpy ride over beautiful green hills and some low mountains. Spain is pretty in this area. It looks like a nice farming land with cattle strewn about little streams, drinking. We stop in the little village of Alcala for a rest, and have coffee and fried potatoes for our breakfast. Then back into our small bus and head for Seville.

We pass a grand old manor house. It's very elegant, so we drive up the long driveway to have a better look. Everyone automatically begins to ask each other "cemetery" questions– measurements, decorations, etc.– and we realize that we are so oriented to this kind of looking and describing that we are hopelessly giggling at our own new habits.

Seville is a pretty city. There are balconies with flower boxes, all with blooms. The Cathedral is either the second or third largest in the world. There is an Easter mass in progress, so we tiptoe through the entire church. The music is wonderful and again, there are flowers everywhere. We couldn't be in a nicer place for Easter. We then walk through half the city, it seems, looking for a restaurant which has been recommended and which turns out not to be so great. So we stop afterwards and buy a sweet at a bakery, and just saunter along taking pictures, stopping to window shop in local squares, and generally taking a nice Easter Sunday stroll.

We leave in mid-afternoon, to head home. We stop in a little town on a river where you can fish, and the restaurant next door will cook your fish, right in front of you. Most of us only have coffee, but it is a serene little spot. We continue past the city of old Cadiz and then ride along the seacoast toward Algeciras, from where one has an incredible view of our Rock. We all stop and take pictures and more pictures and even more. (We could open a store, when we get back). When we do arrive at our hotel, we are all exhausted, and are in bed and asleep, it seems, in minutes.

MONDAY, APRIL 4

Everything in town is still closed for the Easter holiday. It is rainy and cold, but we still go to the cemetery to work on our gravestones. After a few hours we are uncomfortable, and I am so cold that I get the shakes. I finally decide (with the okay from Harold) to walk back to the hotel, and one other person in the group joins me. By the time we get back, we are both a mess and decide that we should just crawl under the covers until we warm up a bit. This takes a few hours and then we feel much better.

So the two of us go back to our jobs in the cemetery. By the time the day is over, everyone else is shivering, also. All of us are now seemingly setting a record for walking on Gibraltar. Too bad there isn't a prize for our exercising.

A good hot dinner and we all fall into bed early.

TUESDAY, APRIL 5

Today it is not raining (they call it misting) but I wear two sweaters, a windbreaker, and a poncho, just in case. This time, we buy sandwiches to suit our tastes since the thought of more cheese and fruit lunches is beginning to take a downward turn for us. I have corned beef on rye, and even a chocolate cupcake. I think I have died and gone to heaven, they are so good.

Spend the afternoon pursuing our gravestone inscriptions and we are getting very good at this. I am called upon to translate one inscription that is in Latin, and although I haven't studied Latin since high school, I manage to make some sense of what is written. My Latin teacher would have been proud of me, although there is no one else to challenge me.

After dinner, two of us go down to the hotel restaurant to top off the day with a fudge sundae. The waitress tells us that she can't serve us "just a dessert" until there are no more customers who might also want fudge sundaes. ???? She brings each of us one anyway but cautions us not to eat it until the restaurant is closing. So we both sit there for several minutes, with our hands over our sundaes, waiting for the doors to close, and then rapidly swallow our dessert and flee. Strangest orders we have ever been given!

WEDNESDAY, APRIL 6

We are off today, so three of us rent a car and decide to drive to Ronda, which is purported to be a wonderful small town, way up in the mountains behind the Costa del Sol. Fortunately, one of us has gone to the bank before we start out because this trip is going to cost us a bit. It is a beautiful drive, except I am not happy on switchbacks or heights, so I look out of the window, at the walls of cliffs, most of the time, instead of looking down at ravines and rivers. We want to stop at all the little mountain villages but have to curb ourselves or we will never get to Ronda in time for lunch.

You come into Ronda over a narrow, very high, shaky bridge, from which no one would ever consider jumping, because you would go on falling forever– it is that high. The town is partially walled, but we all wonder why anyone would want to conquer it. Streets are cobblestoned. There is a bull fighting arena, gorgeous homes with gorgeous flowers, courtyards all over, few cars but horse-drawn carts all over, and of course pretty shops filled with pretty wares of one sort or another, and we are sure the prices are just as pretty, but now the adjective is spelled "pricey". We have a lovely lunch (I am shocked to hear we have to pay extra for our bread and butter) and then try the shops again. Walk around the town until it is time to leave and go back over that awful bridge. I drive the car this time, as it is no job– all down hill. We do stop for coffee at La Linea and then behold, we see our rock not too far in front of us. We are somehow very fond of this rock, and look upon it as our security blanket. The other members of the Earthwatch group have gone over to Tangier (on the hydrofoil which did not have a party on board) and enjoyed their trip. Except one member remarks that it is the worst place she has ever been! Ha! The joys of travelling some place other than the Mall.

THURSDAY, APRIL 7

This will be our last regular full day of work. I really don't mind this cemetery work until my co-worker and I are asked to do a huge monument– measure, record the decorations, etc. It takes us 1- 1/2 hour to stoop and turn sidewise, look upside down– whatever. After finishing this job, I begin to wonder how this will help save the planet or the world, or philosophically what am I doing here. Then I think it is certainly better than collecting garbage for a living, and so I stop complaining.

FRIDAY, APRIL 8

Now this is really the last day for our Gibraltar experience. Two of us are asked if we will go back to the cemetery just one more time, since there are still three tall statues left to "be done". We wonder why the two of us are born so tall? Now we know. So back we go for a few hours, and then sit down and have our lunch. The "cemetery" cat comes to visit us one last time. We wonder if he will miss the tidbits that we have been giving to him. I would like to take him home with me, to a happier place to live, but he doesn't have a passport. Poor Pussycat!

In the afternoon we are driven on a tour of the rest of Gibraltar that we have never seen. We actually go inside the rock (there are 67 miles of road in there) but we are only allowed just so far. We stop at St. Michael's cave and are awed by the vastness of it, plus all those stalagmites. Europa Point gives a great view across to Africa, and a great view of the Straits, and if you turn around, another great view of the Gibraltar harbor and of course, another angle of the rock. There is a long tunnel through the rock, and on the other side of the rock is the town of Catalan Bay.

Of course, there are the Barbary Apes, which is why we really came here in the first place. Obviously, we find them enchanting until they start climbing in the windows of our bus and trying to grab our backpacks or purses. We are laughing and screaming at the same time. They would love to find some food but they are thwarted with all the zippers on the backpacks and purses. The driver finally persuades them– by shouting so loudly— to vacate, and they scamper out the windows, and sit on the stonewall next to us, looking sorrowful and unhappy, and we are not fooled and quickly move on.

That night we go back to Catalan Bay for our "Goodbye Dinner" which is excellent, and we have a fine time. Including a special fudge cake.

"The Rock"—our cementary below.

Cemetery with airstrip next to it.

Chapter 4: Rocks of Gibraltar

Our worksite.

The open grave.

Looking down into a grave!

Back to work.

Still wondering.

It did rain one day.

Hello! (Barbary ape)

I'm so hungry.

Why I really came here!

Good-bye, good times!

CHAPTER 5

1989: POLAND
COMPETITION AND COEXISTENCE
IN PREDATOR'S COMMUNITY

INTRODUCTION

On the border between Poland and Russia is the Bialowieza (pronounced Bee-a-low-vee-asha)- National Park, Man and Biosphere Reserve, and World Heritage. Now that you know that, is there more? It is also called the "Mecca of Biologists". It is also the last primeval forest left in Europe. The forest is filled with wolves, lynxes, foxes, eagles, martens, badgers, weasels, and buzzards. The village is old-fashioned with wooden houses and lots of white stork nests on the barn roofs. We will investigate the functioning of the unique community of predators in the forest, their diets, and breeding performance. We will also note prey remains. This project will form a base for new conservation and management rules of endangered species of predators, here in Poland and throughout Europe

THURSDAY, JUNE 29

Ann and I were roommates at college. Now the two of us are on route to London and then on to Warsaw, Poland, to work on a project as volunteers in Poland's Primeval Forest. This will be a true adventure for us, working in a Communist country, which neither of us has ever experienced before. We are unable to speak the language, and also cannot read the language. We also are hoping that our scientist-in-charge of the project, Wlodizimerz Jedrzejewski, has a nickname, which we will be able to pronounce.

FRIDAY, JUNE 30

We land in Warsaw and get through customs quickly, but then have to go to another building to change U.S. money into zlotys. Unbeknownst to us, the moneychangers will not accept traveler's checks– just American dollars. A nice man in line behind us offers to take our traveler's checks and gives us $50. Phew! Then there are two different rates– communist and non-communist. We finally settle all this and enter the city to find a cab to our hotel. They have our reservations! We are given a nice room where we wash up and rest, and then go downstairs for dinner. The food is very good, and very cheap. Outside the hotel windows are a group of protesters, who are protesting something, and are noisy and we get nervous. But then white-helmeted police arrive and chase these people away with fire hoses. Welcome to Poland!

SATURDAY, JULY 1

It's Saturday morning and after a good night's sleep, and a good European breakfast (cold cuts, cheeses, fruit, eggs, and Polish pastries), we wait to be picked up by our leader– whom we decide to call Wojac, right away, before he will pronounce it the correct way and we will be tongue-tied for the rest of the trip. He does arrive, with a young woman named Judy, who will be the third Earthwatcher in the group. The three of us walk around the Old Town of Warsaw while Wojac goes off to the airport to pick up our fourth team member, Zora. We have a lovely walk through cobblestoned streets, busy squares with shops and restaurants, somber old gray churches, and signs of continuing restoration. Damage from WWII is extensive and it is taking years to restore the city.

When Zora arrives with Wojac, we take a trolley ride out of town, to the church where Solidarity started. Solidarity was the name of the movement led by Lech Walesa, to try to turn Poland away from Communism and into more of a democracy. The police had murdered one of the priests of this church and threw his body in the nearby river. This is just one of the incidents which kept occurring during this very unsettled time in Poland. There is a strong underground movement threatening the government and the very life of the people in the country. There is a small grave for the young priest, decorated each day with fresh flowers, and inside are a few remains of his belongings– relics of his martyrdom. We gladly buy little pins, which we attach underneath our coat collars, which later on prove to be a very good idea.

After lunch back in the hotel, we go to the train station for the five-hour trip to Bialowieza (Bee-al-o-vee-a'sia). There are two young girls in the compartment with us who are nice and at least they can stumble through some English words, whereas the four of us sit there totally mute. Suddenly a fight erupts in the aisle outside our open compartment, between a very large man and two young policemen. We remain totally mute and also horrified. The large man finally is beaten and thrown to the floor with a ripped shirt and a bloody nose.

I don't ask the others, but I am beginning to wonder what I am doing here and if I will ever get back home alive.

We arrive at our little town, after dark and are escorted to our rooms, which supposedly were once part of the Tsar's Hunting Lodge. I think we all would have settled for a bench in the park after our long day of sights and scenes. The light in our rather bare little room is very dim, and fearing it would go out any minute, we quickly get into our pajamas, cover up with warm blankets, and go right to sleep.

SUNDAY, JULY 2

I have to be wakened from a deep sleep the next morning. We put on clean clothes, over our dirty bodies and go racing off to breakfast. Of course we are late so we grab a muffin and go out to the horse-drawn carriage to go visit the forest. Carriage is a fancy name for what was really a wagon. On our ride through the village and lovely fields of blue flowers, we can see the Russian military installation over at the border of the two countries. We are warned to stay away from that area nearest to the border. As we approach the forest, there is a guard's little building on our left, which looks exactly like a little box, in which a nut-cracker-kind of man, with a uniform and a moustache, straight out of a fairy tale, is waiting for us to stop and show our passports, etc. We sit spellbound as he looks through our papers, nods his head, retreats back into his box, and slams his door shut. Does he live there all day? We wonder since there are seldom any other people who are allowed in the forest.

Inside the fence of the forest are some "grids" which have already been earmarked for our work. A grid is just a marked area– in this case with little flags. At one point, we stop to watch a young ornithologist climb a tree and in the branches, there is a big raptor's nest. There are two baby buteos in the nest. The birdman picks the two birds up and puts them in his big bag so they won't jump out. The fear is that stone martens often climb trees to steal the birds from their nest and bring them down to feed their own families. While the birds are in his bag, he cleans the nest of their pellets to test for what these birds have eaten. Here we begin to get into the prey/predator picture. The young man then puts the little raptors back in their nest, climbs down the tree, and disappears down the forest path. We then continue on our ride through marshes and woods looking for more of the grids, and get muddy and filthy all over again. We get back to the cart, and since we have forgotten to bring our lunch and are slowly starving to death, we ride back to the science building where the cafeteria is, have a good meal, and go over to Wojac's office in the Institute. He shows us all the animals and explains why they are being studied, and that they are cared for very well. We question him. But they do look okay. We then go back to our rooms and take SHOWERS and wash our hair, and feel much better. Dinner, at 8 p.m., is fine, but a bit late for our usual schedule, but we will get used to this new regime.

MONDAY, JULY 3

Today we go to work. We pick up our bicycles at the Institute. A wagon is going to follow us into the forest, with the traps for the animals and the other stuff we need. Inside the forest, we break into two teams– I'm with Judy and Ann is with Zora. We place the traps accordingly to where the flags are, push the mice into the cage, and load five different grids. Tie ribbons around a tree nearby (not yellow!) and remove the flags we had left before, as markers. Now everything looks less staged. We sit and have our lunch and go back to work until we run out of traps.

Back to the Institute, and then Ann and I ride into the village. There is not much here. We stop to visit with Wojac's family and meet his little daughter. She is so sweet, but looks so fragile and pale. We are served gooseberries and cookies, which are delicious. Wojac is at a Solidarity meeting and when he comes home, he does not discuss it with us. The village is so quiet when we leave; no cars, no lights in houses, no dogs, and only one cat.

There is so little to buy in the stores here that if people did not grow their own vegetables, etc., I don't know how they would survive. Back to the Institute for dinner at 9:30 p.m. (aren't we getting cosmopolitan?) and then to our rooms. Ann kills a huge black spider, which is on one wall, and I am sure it was he who bit my finger when I was asleep, and that is now very sore.

TUESDAY, JULY 4

Get to the Institute about 9:30 a.m. and set off, in teams, to check on the traps that we have set in the grids, yesterday. These are have-a-heart traps (in Polish?) so there are no dead animals. Each trap is set with a piece of beet, some water soaked cotton, and the bait is one white mouse. Judy and I, with one of the staff, are responsible for all the grids to the left of the entry path into the forest; Ann and Zora, with their staff member do the right hand side. We finish first, having changed the water, put in a new tidbit of food, and cleaned out the running-around room in the cage, and of course talked to the mouse, who is still there, and has not met with any intruders. We decide we would make good motel room cleaners! We sit on a log in the forest and have our lunch, which is a decidedly different kind of dining room. Birds singing, small things buzzing around, things dropping from the tall trees... there is no need for talk, we are being entertained by nature. We pedal back to the Institute, about 4 p.m. Then we go to Wojac's house in the village, where he tells us about everything he and his wife are studying here in Bialowieza. I am so tired by now; I really don't care what anyone is doing in Bialowieza. We all finally are allowed to get on our bikes and pedal back to the Institute. It doesn't take us long to collapse into bed.

WEDNESDAY, JULY 5

Today, we all agree that we are beginning to "get" the picture of this whole project. Have coffee in our rooms before getting our breakfast at 8 a.m. Then right over to the Institute to pick up our bikes (two of which had been repaired, thank goodness), fill our baskets with supplies, and we are off to the forest on our own. We all work fast and do a good job. Unfortunately, we lose two field mice, and one white mouse. We vow revenge, but at whom? Judy and I get back about 2 p.m. and Wojac gives us the rest of the afternoon off. We buy some cards, etc. at the shop here in the park, and then go into the village, and buy a pair of gloves.

We also take pictures of the oldest house in the town, where a retired Russian general lives. The yards of the houses here are large and well tended, due to the fact that one grows as many vegetables and fruits possible because food tends to be sparse and also expensive. There are two churches – one at each end of town– the Russian Orthodox and the Greek Orthodox. We go inside one of them and are amazed and impressed that there are no plastic statues anywhere. The altar is made completely of tree branches and the wall sconces too. These people are really Beylo-Russians (white Russians). Their houses look quite Swedish, and we are told that this is because, at one point in history, the Scandinavians invaded these lands and often left marks of their homeland in the form of architecture. Even the mustard-colored paint on these houses is reminiscent of Scandinavian colors. At the other end of town– the shopping end– is a variety store and a food store. The variety store has a few toys and the rest is electrical equipment– fuses, cords, and a few teapots. There are a few face creams and hair curlers in the variety store, but not much else.

We return to our Institute in the park in time for dinner at 4:30 pm and then back to our rooms and find HOT WATER. We take showers, wash some clothes and sit around and read. There is a tour of the Museum, but we stay in our rooms, relax and catch up with each other's lives.

THURSDAY, JULY 6

Up, up and away for another day in the forest. I enjoy working with Judy so much because, being a nurse, she has an innate kindness toward all creatures– us humans and animals alike. I giggle as she talks to the mice in our cages, telling them that room service has finally arrived, and that we will vacuum their little room and renew their food and water, and that they are supposed to be quiet and make no sound so that the predators will not find them.

Back to the institute, we all report and then all four of us ride to the hotel on the far side of town where we exalt in finding COKE. Later that day, we have a lecture on Wolves, which is good but scary; there are many wolves in Poland and some live in our forest. We also are told that tomorrow will be our last day of motel service to our mice, and then on Saturday we are to pick them up and all of us return to the Institute together. We are delighted, as we have all become rather fond of these four-footed friends with whom we have visited every day.

SUNDAY, JULY 7

Another day in the woods– basically the same routine. Provide "room service" for the mice and tell them we will be back tomorrow to bring them home to the Institute. Pedaling between the grids, we see a family of wild boars, parents and four children. They run off across the path, but we have a good look at them. At lunch, we sit on another tree log, and I put down my Swiss Army Knife, after using it to cut bread. I walk away from lunch without picking it up again.

The next day the knife is gone, and although I really depend on that knife, I figure that the only person in the forest that day is a local farmer. I had checked with the "Nutcracker" guard at the entrance to the forest. I decide the local farmer probably needs it more than I do. I can get another.

Have dinner at the Institute that night with the head of the facility, Dr. Puchuk, who talks to us about his study of shrews, and the other work that's been done here over the years. He interestingly tells us that the Russians not only call their side of the forest THEIRS, but also the Polish side THEIRS. Because this is one of the favorite hunting areas of the Tsars, he does say that the Russian director and he discuss problems concerning the forest. The Russian area is a semi- protected area while ours is fully protected. He admits there are still poachers. When the Doctor refers to the Russians, he always rolls his eyes to the ceiling, which is quite funny.

After the talk with the Doctor, we are all taken to a Lithuanian Dance Festival outside our village of Bialowiezia to a nearby meadow. The troupe is composed of students who won a prize last year. Costumes are lovely with embroidered blouses, full skirts, red boots and hair ribbons. The boys are in tunics with belts and also red boots. Russian instruments include a huge balilika. Nearby, a fire is built and we all adjoin to that area, and sit on logs. Then there is more dancing and singing– a most memorable performance, by a stream, in this misty meadow, and a lovely new moon.

SATURDAY, JULY 8

Today is free and its free-the-mice day. We are up early, have breakfast, and are picked up by two grad students who will go with us to pick up our little white four-footed friends and take them back to the Institute. One mouse has escaped, two mice, to put it gently, have gone on to mouse heaven, but everyone else is accounted for. Boy, are we glad to no longer be responsible for these tiny lives.

We stop at a restaurant in town for lunch, and then go back to our rooms to wash our very dirty "forest clothes". There is no washing machine, so we take turns stomping on our slacks/jeans in the bathtub. None of us has ever done this before and we all end up laughing until tears run down our cheeks. Zora and Ann have disappeared and when they return, they tell us that they sneaked back into the forest so they could go over toward the Russian zone, to see what they could see. They saw two Russian soldiers patrolling along the border, with rifles over their shoulders. That was enough. They sneaked back the way they had come, terrified of being seen, and then assumed heroic attitudes for being so clever. None of us are impressed!

That evening, we go back to the hotel across town where they have a Coke machine, and go in the hotel where the local teenagers are having a dance. Absolutely no different from what we see in the U.S. It must be a disease! And then our group tastes our first Polish beer, which is very good. We are learning.

SUNDAY, JULY 9

It's Sunday, so we go to church. We choose the Russian Orthodox one and arrive at 10 a.m. There are no pews and no place to sit down. The church is beautifully ornate, with candelabras of candles. Young girls replace the burnt-out candles, or tilted ones. Everyone kisses pictures and statues– all the time standing. For the very old people, their families have brought little carpets on which the elderly kneel. A choir sings from a room behind us. We stand for 1-1/2 hours and leave before communion is offered. The whole service must take over 3 hours. Outside, old ladies sit on benches, to rest their feet, and then go back into the church. The priest has yet to give his sermon. One of the bench ladies indicates that her friend is 94 years of age. And she stands or kneels for all that time! Wow!!!!!

We have lunch back at the Park and since it is very hot today, everyone goofs off and does next to nothing. Actually, we never seem to run out of talk– comparing our lives, etc, before Poland, etc. etc.

MONDAY, JULY 10

We had a fierce storm last night, but at least it cools our rooms. We sleep fitfully, but are up at the regular time and Ann and I are off to the Village to help Wojac and his wife Beruska with some paperwork to do with the project. We do a layout for an ad, edit several papers, and catalog raptor periodicals for their files. It is very hot in their house and I get punchy over the titles under which we are filing papers; i.e. Eleanora's Falcon, Misfired Eggs, etc. etc. Ann and I concoct a story about the Winks and the Rostows, who write all fourteen articles about the Falcons. Beruska thinks we have gone crazy (maybe she is right?) but with the heat and all this foreign information we are working with, we do feel a bit crazy. We leave about 2:30 pm, pick up the other Earthwatchers who have been working in the lab, and have our lunch together and then back to our rooms.

After dinner, Dr. Puchek gives us a lecture on the bison– the great "draw" at Bialowieza– which instead turns into a lecture on politics in Poland. He is fascinating, but also an endless talker. Eventually, he does a short paragraph on the bison that roams through our Park. Then we are excused because there is another big storm approaching, and we need to get back to our rooms before it starts to rain.

TUESDAY, JULY 11

We get to breakfast late, and find the room already filled. We wait and are eating a piece of bread, when Wojac bursts into the room to tell us that a herd of bison has been seen nearby. We run back to our rooms to get boots because we will be in a muddy area and will need them. We get the boots, and get into the van and head off to the forest. We arrive at the spot, get out of the van and sure enough, we are in wet, humid woods, glades and down along railroad tracks. We trudge for what seems to be 5 miles, and see one bison. We are sweaty, and hungry, and tired. We give up the search. Go back to our rooms and get out of our boots. By now we are ready to eat the bark off the trees. Instead we go to the dining room where they have saved us some food. Phew! Manna from heaven. We did see a big antlered male deer on the railroad tracks, but he hardly counted at that point.

Beusha calls and has made arrangements for us to visit a sculptoress– a lady who is well known in the area. We get on our bikes and ride out to a country cottage. Right out of a fairy tale. Since I also indulge in sculpture, I am amazed at the work she does with so few tools. I ask her if I may send her some of my extra tools (which I actually do when I get back to the States) and she is delighted. We each buy a piece of her work– I buy a small moose, carved from wood, and am totally pleased.

Back to the Institute, dinner, and then the four of us catch up on our journals and our postcards. No storm tonight.

WEDNESDAY, JULY 12

We all had a fitful night's sleep, so get up early, make it to the dining room for breakfast, and I, for one, am not feeling too well. It happens that this is the morning that I am assigned to the lab to do "Scats". This is the term for digging through feces of animals to see what they have ingested. The idea does not sit very well with my stomach feeling the way it does, but amazingly, once one gets into this dicey job, it is fascinating what you can find out about Prey and Predator. I would never think about finding bones or hair would cause such excitement. All this stuff has been frozen, so there is no smell. Thank goodness.

After lunch (only a little sandwich for me), we are to hear a lecture on Conservation. We also go to the park museum to meet one of the curators who shows us pictures of how this place looked when the Russians owned it. Our hotel (motel?) does actually look like a Hunting Lodge, which it was. It even has one of those onion-type steeples and is charming.

When dinner is over, about 6:30 pm, we are invited to Wojac's and Begushas house for a last night party. It is lovely, with little cakes, a pudding, juice, and salted sticks. Also, lima beans as a snack. We Americans wonder where our host has gotten enough sugar to make the cakes, since the shelves in the local stores have no such things. After the eating part of the party, we are shown pictures of Wojac's and her work at the Institute. Their little daughter, Helena, sits on Judy's lap and cries out to be rescued by her parents. It is so sad to see her so afraid of foreigners. To our surprise, we are then given presents– tablemats and a runner, good reprints of animals by a Polish artist and lastly we are shown a PBS film about the Bison at Bialowieza. We are very moved by their tribute to and for us. We get back late, and put off our packing until tomorrow.

THURSDAY, JULY 13

Today is our good-bye day. We have breakfast at a sensible hour— 8:30 a.m. and then we are driven over to the Reserve, where some animals are kept, as in a zoo. We see the bison, up close, since we missed them the other day, in the forest. But now it is great to see other Tarpans, which are all remnants of the pure wild horses that roamed Europe and Asia centuries ago. They have one dark stripe down their backs. Quite a sight.

Back to the Institute to be served a little tea party out on the lawn, for all the staff people and us their visitors. All the ladies are so fascinated by our Western ways, and I think they are   stunned when we get up to help clear away the plates. We have no way to communicate except with charades or shaking our heads, no or yes, or pantomiming. It's amazing how quickly we all catch on. Dr. Puchek is there, of course, and invites each of us into his office to talk with him a minute, and then to sign his guest book. We have our snack for the morning, so go   back to our rooms, finish packing, and are ready when the van arrives at 2:30 pm to begin our journey back to Warsaw.

We stop at the first town to buy some food for our trip and there is nothing available or at least   travel-worthy. As we leave this town, we are impressed by the modern Russian Orthodox Church, which has a 3-dimensional cross hanging in the center of the sanctuary. It is gorgeous.

We go to a larger town– really a city– Bialystok– which has a supermarket.   These shelves are also basically empty. How do these people survive? We do buy vegetables from private people who are selling off the sidewalks. One man gives Ann a bouquet of phlox. When Wojac takes us to a gift shop where we buy at a crazy pace, and the owners decide we are all madmen. We buy blouses, wooden eggs, aprons, and pillowcases– at foolishly low prices. Next, we go to the railroad station to buy our tickets for tomorrow. The hotel in which we will spend the night is near the well-known privet marshes. It is large and not very clean and inhabited by a group of men, who are loud, slovenly and quite drunk, and even come and use OUR bathroom. Wojac's room is near us, which makes us feel safer, so we sit in his room until 9 p.m., then tiptoe down the hall to our own rooms, quickly lock the door and go right to sleep!

FRIDAY, JULY 14

We have to get up early and prepare for a long day. We see two Russian bunkers in the forest as we drive past. The Tsars built the bunkers in 1900 to repel the Germans. They were blown up two weeks later by the Germans. Also, there is a trench remaining around the bunkers, now filled with water and acting like a moat. We take some back roads through little rural villages and then we stop at one of the houses (a friend of Wojac's) and have coffee and a berry pie. We sit outside and there is a fawn in the meadow that comes to us to be petted. On we go and stop at a hill, which has a monument on top of it, to a Polish soldier who held the hill while his comrades retreated, and then the Germans killed him but the others escaped. In one village, we pass a large hay wagon heavily loaded to its very top but one could see the heads of two women poking through the hay, waiting with their pitch forks to help unload the hay when they get to where they are going.

We finally get to the train station to board for Warsaw. The four Earthwatchers sit together in a compartment. The conductor comes to collect our tickets and he is not very friendly. Then he sees my Solidarity pin on my collar, looks out into the corridor for passer-byes, and finding none, comes back in, turns his lapel outside for us to see HIS Solidarity pin. We all smile together and all is fine between us.

The ride into Warsaw seems endless and we do not arrive there until after 10 p.m. We take a taxi to Berusha's parents house– Mr. and Mrs. Sticert. They think we are not coming but still have our supper waiting... wonderful stewed apples, bread, sliced meat, rice cakes, coffee… a huge feast for us since we have had a very long trip

SATURDAY, JULY 15

Our morning is resplendent with a true Polish breakfast of cheeses, salami, pickles, white cheese, bread, coffee and platefuls of other delicacies. Mr.Stircet takes us to his backyard to see his animals; two cats, a dozen chickens, including little ones, geese, and two cages of nutria. He grows flowers and vegetables. The yard is very crowded, but these people have to grow things to survive. After our tour, we go into Warszawa (!) by bus and then a little train.

Poor Wojac suffers through all our shopping sprees in a department store and then we walk over to the Old Town and go to the Palace. We have tickets for 12:30 pm. We begin to understand what the Polish people went through during the war as we see a full restoration still at work. Many countries, including Germany, helped finance this restoration, which was not completed until 1984. In the Palace, we have to wear paper shoes because the parquetted floors are so gorgeous. After the Palace, we walk around the Square and find a restaurant for lunch. I have my favorite pork and beer and also a black currant drink, which is delicious. We decline going to the theater as we like sitting in the Square and watching the people, while we have coffee. At 8 p.m., we go to Wojac's church with him (our idea) and there is a lot of up-and-down ritual, but the church is ornate and restful. We go back to his in-law's house, find a little spread of food, supplied by our hosts, and then off to bed.

SUNDAY, JULY 16

We rise early, have breakfast and re-pack. A cab arrives at 10 a.m. to take us to the airport. We are too early to board, so check our luggage and go back into town. Ann buys jewelry and I buy a painting. Later, it takes us 1-1/2 hours to get through security. The custom people are not very friendly and we have the feeling they resent us. Who knows! At a kiosk in the terminal, I buy an amber pendant– amber being the choice gem because there is an abundance of it in these countries. Finally we are on the plane to London. We shepherd a young boy through Heathrow, as this is his first trip out of Poland. Then over to our hotel for the night, and a scrumptious dinner of roast beef, salad, wine and espresso.

MONDAY, JULY 17

Homeward bound on British Air at 11 am.

Hello!

We start here… the entrance to our park.

Chapter 5: Competition and Coexistence

Bison in the park.

What do you do after dinner? Walk your geese home!

Chapter 5: Competition and Coexistence

A well in the a backyard.

Halt! Who goes there? The "Nutcrakcer" guardhouse.

Delivery person of traps and other supplies.

Into the forest.

We are treated to a Lithuanian dance in the meadow.

Our leader, Wojac.

A road shrine on a road to Warsaw.

Notice the two ladies sitting in the hay.

Chapter 5: Competition and Coexistence

Russian Orthodox Church.

CHAPTER 6

1988: MADAGASCAR
RINGTAILS

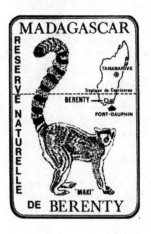

INTRODUCTION

It is necessary to understand something about Madagascar before joining this group from Earthwatch. It is the fourth largest island in our world. It was a bit of the African Continent, until about 200 million years ago, when it cut loose into the Mozambique Channel and has remained where it is since that date. It can only be described as an amazing place to visit, since it is known to be unique in both animal and plant life, which you will never see anywhere else. There are 8000 plant specimens known, some 80% are native to this island only; 98% of the reptiles, half the birds and bats, and all of the non-flying land animals except those brought in by people. It boasts deserts and forests and gorgeous seacoasts. In the capitol of Antananarivo, there is recognizable city life, but there are still women washing their clothes in the river. This country is also well known for being one of the first countries to have established nature reserves. Thank goodness because half the forests have been cut down for firewood, and the land that is left is badly unprotected from people and other hazards.

And so, after landing in the capitol city, staying in an hotel for the night, we were to take a flight the next morning, to the southern tip of the island. We would then drive to the Berenty Reserve. Our quarters on a sisal plantation were given to this Reserve.

Berenty, itself is a small private forest isolated on a sisal plantation. A large tract of spiny desert had been bulldozed in order to plant sisal. When the owners of the land, the De Heaulmes, saw that the bulldozing part of the project was going to interfere with a beautiful tamarind forest bordering on the Mandrave River, they stopped the project and turned this forest into a Preserve. They left a path through the forest so that cattle herds could come to the river to drink, and they left the rest of the forest to the lemurs and the white Sifaka lemurs, who were also living there. Scientists and students have been coming here for years, to pursue their studies. Tourists also have arrived, and are part of our study. We will address new concerns about their presence.

The proposal for this trip is to study the range and territorial behavior of troops of ringtails, which live in an isolated forest on the southernmost area named the Berenty Preserve on the island of

Madagascar. Our leader will be Dr. Allison Jolly, from Princeton University, in New Jersey, USA.

Lemurs travel, and live in "troops" and there are many troops in the forest of Berenty. Volunteers will be assigned to each troop and will follow the lemurs through out their usual day, from getting up in the morning (they sleep in the same tree each day, but have another tree, in another part of the preserve for their waking hours). They return to their night sleeping tree at dusk and wake up by dawn. These will be our hours of study– from dawn to dusk—five days in a row, to study their patterns of behavior.

Examples of the behaviors, which we will be recording, are the territorial conflicts between two troops, reaction to calls from neighboring troops, and the survival of newborns. We will compare groups of food-enhanced groups lemurs who feed not only on forest vegetation, but enjoy snacks from the staff as well as visitors, to those lemurs who studiously adhere only to the vegetation.

There will be appearances of another type of lemur– the Sifaka– which is a large, furry white lemur who has short front legs and longer back legs which results in a leaping sort of moving, which sometimes looks as though the animal is dancing. It is very funny and astonishing to watch this movement. You look and look and think this animal should just stop performing, and then you realize that this is his genuine way of moving from place to place.

So, off we go!

FRIDAY, OCTOBER 12

We are finally ready to leave Nairobi and head over to Madagascar to meet up with our Earthwatch team. The plane is divided into two parts-the front has a sign saying Mauritius and halfway back the sign reads Madagascar. That's also how the luggage is put on the plane. We wonder if, at the stop at Mauritius, if the front part of the plane is unscrewed from the back, and left there, and the back part goes on to our destination? A few of us get the giggles about this. We set down in the Comoros Island to pick up more passengers, some of whom look shabby, and we wonder who will be our seatmates for the next leg of the trip. Now it is a crowded flight but fast, and then we arrive at the airport in Antananarivo. We take a taxi into the town, past rice paddies, and oxen carts carrying bales of hay. There are rickshaws, and a man walking a pig, on a rope. This is indeed another world.

We stay one night at a hotel with modest accommodations but we are so tired we would sleep on a park bench if necessary. There will be a delay in our flight today, so it is time to see the sights in this city, tomorrow.

SATURDAY, OCTOBER 13

The city awakens to the sound of barking dogs and crowing roosters. After breakfast, we hire a driver to show us around this incredible– to us– capital. First we go to the Zoma Market, which is huge, and I haggle over a tablecloth (I can't believe I am doing this) but the driver insists this is the normal procedure. Far be it for me to mess up the economy. We are taken outside the city where there are the rice paddies, and women washing clothes and themselves in the river. At the President's Palace, we are not allowed out of the car, but take pictures through the window. Our driver talks about the Zebu– an animal who is new to us– and he tells us that two oxen are Zebu and three, four, or five oxen are also Zebu. We decide to change the subject.

In the afternoon we start out again, and go to the Queen's Palace where we are also not allowed. We suspect we are not to go into any public buildings, but we get out of the car, and casually walk through the whole palace. On to the Zoo, where we see our first lemurs, including two babies who are no larger than two field mice. I would love to take one home, but am dissuaded quickly by the driver throwing his hands in the air and almost snarling.

SUNDAY, OCTOBER 14

Today we are at the airport by 7:30am for our flight to Fort Dauphin. We arrive and are surprised to see a cinder-block building, the size of a garage, with one door. This is the terminal. We see no Earthwatch person, so gather our luggage and sit on a stonewall. The Earthwatcher lady arrives at 9:30 am and we finally feel official. We now wait for the others to arrive on their later flight. Finally we are all driven to a small hotel (1 use the term loosely) for another day. By this time, the whole Team 1 is together (about 24 of us) and we have time to get to know each other. There is a nice lunch on the patio of the hotel in the afternoon, and then a leisurely buffet later. Everyone is tired, but pleased that we are almost ready to see our own wonderful lemurs.

MONDAY, OCTOBER 15

A beautiful day ahead of us. We are being treated to an outing in an area known as Sainte Luce. It is a long bumpy ride in a closed Land Rover, but it sure cuts down on the dust. First stop is a field of yellow insect-eating plants called Nepenthes. Then on to a wild cove to see the waves crashing against the rocks. The villagers come to stare at us, while we pick up shells and driftwood. The beach is covered with true dugout pirogues (like our Indian canoes), all hand-made. Some have built-in baskets for fish.

There is still wild surf here, and great rock formations out in the water and we will always remember this as the real Madagascar. Back through fields, to the spot where we started, there is a tablecloth spread for us on the sand and a picnic of skewered fish, rice salad, sliced roast beef and bananas. We are beginning to think we are not here to work at all. We are here on some wonderful holiday.

Now we are transported (by pirogues) across the channel to an island that is a protected reserve. Up a small mountain we have a view of the entire peninsula. On the way down, there is a sprig of wild white orchids hanging from a tree. I am sure I am in wonderland. As we walk on the beach we are alerted to be quiet. There in a tree on the beach, is a boa constrictor wound around a branch-fast asleep. We are VERY quiet. We finally get back to our picnic spot, where the young waiter-boys have bottles of beer and Cokes for us. Two of us go out into the surf so we can say we swam in the Indian Ocean. After a while it begins to get dark, so back we go to the hotel– we cross 27 bridges– all shapes and sizes, but however, they did not cross any water. Go figure?

TUESDAY, OCTOBER16

If we don't get to Berenty soon, all of us will go back to Sainte Luce and stay there forever! But we leave at 9 a.m. to head there. We stop at a market, (just to look) and move on to look at some tombstones. Then we stop to examine a rare aloe– actually extinct– and finally, we arrive at Berenty. The room assignments are mixed up, but nevertheless, we are here with the lemurs and whatever else comes along.

We walk around part of Berenty and see our first real lemurs both ring-tailed, some white ones. A bus picks us up, to take us to the dining room. This is pleasant and we enjoy our first dinner here in the wild. Allison Jolley, our world-famous professor of lemurs, is there with us, and talks about our regimen starting tomorrow. She is a good teacher and a fine scientist, and we, like prancing horses, are ready to go.

WEDNESDAY OCTOBER 17

We're up early to catch the bus by 7 a.m. to the dining room for breakfast. Then we are off to the trails. Allison explains how we keep our charts. We go down one of the paths and find two troops (Scuffy and Dog). Each troop from now on will have a name. At this point Scuffy and Dog members are having a confrontation. It's interesting to watch all their tactics. We don't interfere. We spend the morning on the paths, having little lectures all the while, and we are beginning to "get it". We go back to the dining room for lunch and conversation, and then back to our rooms to organize our lives for this coming five days of real work. The bus returns for us at 3:30 pm and we go back on the trails for our last "accompanied" lessons.

Dinner is late, but extra special because there are two birthdays today amongst our team. Happy time. To bed early because the electricity goes off early here, to save the power.

THURSDAY, OCTOBER 18

When we arrive at the dining room, the Breakfast Club has already arrived. This is a small group of very spoiled lemurs that arrive each morning to pick up snacks from the kitchen door. They also then hang out at the front door hoping one of us will give them a banana. We are told not to do this. It is showering early today, but after breakfast, it simply turns cloudy. We follow the trail along the fence to get a sense of the limits at Berenty and also the tourist area. On the road along the fence we see our first Sifaka. Their front legs are so short that they hop on their back legs across spaces and kind of to the beat of the Mexican Hat Dance. They are large and white, and are both amusing and spectacular to watch.

At lunch we are sorted into our official teams, starting at 5 am tomorrow. We do chores around the preserve in the afternoon, then dinner, then race back to our rooms to ready for our VERY early wake-up call.

P.S. Madagascar is world known for its wealth of butterflies. We are seeing lots of them here at Berenty, but don't have time to stop and categorize them.

FRIDAY, OCTOBER 19

This is our first day of rising at 4:30am to start tracking. We each go to our own assigned troop, who live, eat, sleep, in one particular tree. It takes our group about ten minutes to walk there, and we tiptoe as we near the tree in case the lemurs are not quite up and about. Don't worry, we find out– they are instantly aware that we are there. Now begins a routine that none of us will ever forget and will probably never get used to. We have to wait until all the troop has awakened and are running up and down the tree, stopping to eat a leaf or two, and then climbing down to the ground. We sit and watch and wait. There are three of us in our group. Eventually the lemurs are on the ground and start the next part of their day. This is to walk, jump, leap, talk (they make a funny little meow-ish noise) to each other and continue along and over to what has become, in our country, a junkyard for worn out machines, cars, bicycles, plows, etc. It is in the center of the preserve, and surrounded by a tall wooden fence. In the center of this junkyard is a tall tree with many branches and therefore there are lots of leaves, and jumping-around limbs. AHA! We now know how to name our troop. We are in charge of the Junkyard Troop.

We get a short break to go to the dining room to eat, and leave our charges for a half hour. We are sure the Junkyard guys don't miss us. We return to keep our charts on their movements– every ten minutes~ whether eating, talking, jumping around or just sleeping. When we return to our spot, the lemurs are all asleep, lying on branches, or in nooks or crannies that they have found. So two of us lie down in "our" spot, too, while one of us keeps watch. We switch off, as long as the lemurs nap, and not until the whole troop wakes up and activity starts, do we sit up again and continue our charts.

Tourists arrive in the afternoon, and wonder what in the world we are doing. We try to explain our presence here but we are not sure they understand. They feed the lemurs bananas, which is allowed, but are warned NEVER to touch them. The lemurs have soft fur like kittens and everyone wants to pet them. But they have a middle "finger" on each hand that is razor sharp and can make a mess of your hand if they claw you.

The three of us break at 5 p.m. to follow the lemurs back to their tree in the forest. The lemurs fool around for a while, but eventually climb up in their evening/night quarters, and are resting soundlessly when we leave.

And now we are free to go and get our dinner, discuss the day. and run back to our rooms to get a night's sleep before that awful wake-up call so early in the morning.

SATURDAY, OCTOBER 20

We find the troop early today, and there are some brown lemurs in "their" tree and also a white shifaka. Why don't they stay in their own trees! Our troop follows their usual route with a few deviations; they go towards the junkyard, but by way of the back of the tourist compound, and also they stray onto the road by the main gate. When they settle in for the day in the junkyard tree, the three of us sit for one and half hours and watch them doing next to nothing. I am about to go up the tree with them and take a nap.

A London journalist, Dan, comes to visit us and we are grateful for the company (but of course, still keep up our monitoring of our children in the tree). Dan has lost his job because he left to come on this trip, which has always been his desire. It's all, and more than, he could have ever dreamt it would be. He is leaving tonight to go back to the "world" and we all promise to keep in touch.

The afternoons around Berenty are always hot and humid, and today is, as they say "in spades". Two of us take the lemurs back to their tree about an hour early, and they don't seem to mind arriving back in the forest where it is a bit cooler. They had just gotten in their branch-beds when there is thunder over the river, and then there is a real downpour. We do not stay to see if the lemurs flee, but we do.

Allison is our dinner partner, and we find we have much to share; we had a landlord, once, who had been married to a scientist with the

Field Museum in Chicago and Allison knew him; Allison is a professor at Princeton, which is near my home town. She advises us on the best Wildlife Organization to which we should all belong, and so forth. It really is a small world, even in Madagascar.

SUNDAY, OCTOBER 21

Today is our day off, but I still wake up at 4:30 a.m. I wonder if the lemurs will miss us this morning. Fat chance! The Breakfast Club is at the dining room when we arrive, and have eaten all the jelly off on one of our Team's plate. But they didn't touch the butter. We are driven to a nearby market, which is crowded and very hot, and all the town people stare at us. They start begging. This is a world performance, and we think we are in a different world here. Wrong! We buy a few things and then head back to the bus to relax in the A/C.

We go to a nice little lake nearby where we all go for a swim. The water feels so good. After a rest and another swim, the Berenty boys bring forth a nice little luncheon for us on a picnic cloth. After another rest and another swim, we get back on the bus, leave this paradise behind and head for Berenty. We arrive to find that there is no water and no electricity. So an evening by flashlight and no shower. One of the team has a disc recording of lemur sounds, and it is so real we think we might bring it to work tomorrow, to see if the lemurs will notice it.

MONDAY, OCTOBER 22

Today we leave to pick up the lemurs and are met by another team who report to us that there is a new member of the Breakfast Club and it is very tiny and seems to have a string for a tail. What a surprise! And we never knew (she) was pregnant. We proceed the way we always do, in spite of the new addition and by mid- morning, have our first encounter, face to face with the latest tourists. They insist on feeding the lemurs as long as the lemurs let them know they are still hungry. We begin to realize how unhealthy this can be for our little creatures. The tourists ignore us and what can we do, but look at them with steely mad eyes. They finally stop.

A little later, one of our team feels ill, and goes back to her room; an hour later the other member goes back to her room, and I am left alone with my charges. Of course the lemurs decide that today, they will take a new route to their tree. So I am left with them alone in the forest and trust they will not lead me astray. They don't. I wait by their tree until they are bedded down, then leave (I do not kiss them goodnight, but they did bring me through the forest safely) and go to dinner.

TUESDAY, OCTOBER 23

This will be the second day of our thirteen-hour tracking, and we are nervous as we wonder how we will do it. A number of the team have been laid low with some sort of cold or stomach upset, so some of us will be substituting for others. On our team, we of course go to the usual "tree" and find it empty. Where have they all gone? We continue down the path, further into the woods and we run into another team who mistakes "ours" for "theirs". Good heavens— the war of the lemurs and who owns whom.

We finally straighten out the run-aways and they in turn return to their usual route and the Junkyard troop ends up in their spot amidst all the junk, and we settle down for our daily chores of watching and waiting. It begins to get boring by lunchtime, and so we stiffly get up and take turns going to eat. (We can never leave these rascals unattended). The lunch does not, however, fire up our energy, and when I return, I am about to nod off when one of the team opens a jar of Trader Joe's peanut butter and spreads crackers for the rest of us. That saves us! Delicious! We work until 4:30 p.m., and then even the lemurs seem bored and decide to go back to their tree early. We do not discourage them, follow them, whisper good night when they are all aloft, and race back to our own dinner and drinks and are probably asleep not much later than the lemurs.

Forget one little twist to our daily ritual was when one of the team, with the recording of the cries and mews and the rest of the calls, plays it back to the lemurs while they are quietly relaxing in their Junkyard tree, and they actually answer the recording. Hardly a scientific breakthrough, but it did give me an idea. Explanation later in the journal.

WEDNESDAY, OCTOBER 24

Up again at 4:30 a.m., and we are beginning to think that this is normal behavior. I hope we all get over this when we are back in the States.

The weather, until today, has been warm, but today the tropic heat really sets in. It is really HOT and everything and everyone is drooping. The lemurs walk as if they are wearing heavy shoes– none of this jumping and running. At about 2 p.m., a breeze comes along and now we change our places to get out of the sun, and enjoy the fresh air. We end our duties to the lemurs and race back to our rooms for a shower. There is not an ounce of hot water, but no one minds. We are clean and cool in time for dinner.

Later on in the evening, one of my cohorts leads me to a tall tree on the preserve, which has a "termite line" going up the trunk. We assume the insects use this when they are going aloft, to get food. Halfway up the trunk is a hole from which a lemur is peering at us. He is so tiny and looks like a wise old owl with his feathered arms resting on his windowsill.

THURSDAY, OCTOBER 25

Another long day, so I won't describe it again. I take the late duty today, because I want to try something new, and I am just as happy not to have an audience. I have mentioned before that we had listened to the recording of the lemurs "chattering" back and forth with each other, and I listened to that recording several more times. I have decided I can imitate their voices, and I tried it several times when I was sure that no one was within earshot. Today I decide is going to be the final test.

When it comes time to take the lemurs back to their tree, I stand up and start to do the mews and other little sounds that I have practiced. Believe it or not, the troop stands still for a minute, looking all around, and then when I start to mew again, they take off again, following me, and we talk all the way to the tree. I am ecstatic and just hope they won't expect me to climb the tree and fall asleep on a branch.

They don't. They dutifully climb up to their leafy home, and I shut my mouth and quietly leave them alone. Mission accomplished!!!

FRIDAY, OCTOBR 26

The fact that this will be our last day on duty, we gather our last bit of strength and follow the usual routine. We get to the lemur tree by 5 a.m .and of course, the "kids" have already left. So we walk down the path, farther than usual, and there they are, fooling around and ignoring our disapproval. We gradually get them back on their normal route, ending up at the junkyard, and up over the fence they go and scramble up the tree to spend the rest of the day. We take as many new pictures of our charges to put in our scrapbooks and journals, write down last-minute facts we don't want to forget, exchange addresses and promise to keep in touch.

We drag through dinner without falling asleep and then go back to our quarters to pack, and hopefully get a good sleep.

SATURDAY OCTOBER 27

A troop of lemurs comes thundering across our roof at 5 am. in the morning and that is the end of our sleep. The day is overcast but we all go to breakfast in spite of the gloom and then stand alongside the gate into Berenty to have our team picture taken. Our luggage is already on the bus, so we get on too and off we go. Our first stop is at the home of Allison's maid, who became a good friend when Allison was studying here at the preserve. It is a tiny little house on a dusty road and once inside (we have to sort of squeeze in), it is totally immaculate, and surprise of surprises, she has baked a chocolate cake for us. We wonder how and where she baked it, but of course don't ask. She and Allison sit and converse in Malagasy, which is the official language of Madagascar, while we eat and walk around the premises. Such a treat for us to see a real person in a real house, and we are so pleased with the friendly atmosphere. It is a delight to see a home that is not a shack. We arrive at Fort Dauphin and unload our luggage and ourselves at our hotel.

Allison says we must see the rain forest as part of our appreciation of this island country. It is a long bumpy ride, with bridges (or not) over streams and rivers and the weather is now cold and rainy. Someone has provided a lunch for us, and I sit under the overhang of a big rock and eat, while watching a HUGE millipede and tiny leeches. I do not share my food, and fervently pray that neither of the creatures decide to come closer. At least there are no snakes, but also, there are no orchids. It is very humid, and I admit to myself that I am not an admirer of rain forests.

Back to Fort Dauphin, to clean up and be ready for our final dinner together. Each person is to make a funny little skit about our recent encounters. We toast our leaders and we end our formal time together with good fun and good wishes.

SUNDAY, OCTOBER 28

We have Sunday morning free, so two of us go to a local church, which is another adventure. The church is white clapboard and stands tall in this small town. Inside, the aisle is dusty from the worshippers padding down the dirt floor, barefooted. Lots of chickens walk up and down the aisle, with the people. A mother is feeding her baby in the pew in front of us. The minister is a young man, who of course speaks in Malagasy so we are at a loss in the language department. Even the hymns are in Malagasy. All of a sudden, we hear the beginning of the one hymn we know. It is the Doxology, which we sing at offering time in our own church at home. For a change we can sing along. The offering is not passed; the congregation goes to the altar, row by row and drops coins in a basket.

When we leave the church, the minister, speaking in English, thanks us for coming to the service. We assure him that the pleasure was ours.

Back at the hotel we are hustled over to a nearby restaurant for lunch. The setting is beautiful, on a rock overlooking the sea, and we get a bit nostalgic about leaving this place where we have learned so much and had such a fine visit.

The "terminal" is as we remembered but we are aboard on time and head for Antananarivo, and our connecting flights back to Europe.

Just a regular day in Madagascar.

Washing clothes and yourself in the river.

A house built in a rice paddy.

We fly to Port Dauphin—near to our lemurs.

We take a detour to see a magnificent Madagascar beach.

We drive to the Berenty Preserve where we will "live" with the lemurs.

Our dining hall at Berenty.

And now the ringtail.

And another ringtail.

Another above and below.

Our famous Junkyard Troop Tree.

And the last picture.

CHAPTER 7

1991: GUERNSEY
ATER THE GLACIERS

INTRODUCTION

My grandmother, Emma Tostevin, came to the island of Guernsey from France and in time, married a man from London, George Bond. They later moved to the States, and had four children—three girls and one boy. The boy, Raymond Tostevin Bond was my father.

When I read about the Earthwatch trip to Guernsey to do field work (the name of the project was "Guernsey after the Glaciers), I had to join the group. And so I arrive in St. Peter's Port— the capital of this island, in July of 1991.

The study we are to conduct is the potential consequence of global climate warming on sea level and land areas of Guernsey. "An understanding of past environmental changes, both natural and brought about by human activities is critical in predicting those which may occur in the future." In other words it means we would be studying landscape evolution.

Guernsey is still quite French. The streets have French names, the English language is spoken with a French patois, and the fourteen parishes, which make up the island, have French names.

There are few cars on the island, but regardless, the speed limit is 40 miles per hour and if your conveyance has two, four, six or eight wheels, it makes no difference in the legal pace you must obey.

The famous Guernsey cows are reddish brown with pink noses; while the famous Jersey cows are smaller and are black and white.

The island of Jersey is populated by the "new rich" whereas Guernseyites are referred to as the "old guard". On Sundays, Jerseyites crowd the Catholic churches and the Guernseyites fill the pews of the Methodist churches.

The Jerseyites are called "toads" by their neighbors; in return, the Guernseyites are "donkeys". These names are used mostly at athletic events, which are shared by the two islands throughout the year.

MONDAY, AUGUST 1

The plane leaves for Guernsey a mid-afternoon flight (40 minutes) and we land at the airport on time, and are met by our P.I. (Private investigator/scientist). He gathers us all and we scrunch into our van to drive to St. Peter's Port and down to the harbor where we are registered at a little hotel. We will live here for the next two weeks. It is nice to be situated right on the harbor, but our room is at the back and we look out on the neighbor's roof. We unpack and settle in for a short rest and then a long walk around the town. Our leader, Bob, joins us for dinner in the hotel and tells us about our plans for tomorrow. Then we retreat to our rooms to sleep.

TUESDAY, AUGUST 2

The next morning, after breakfast, we are driven to the Guernsey Museum, where Bob has his office, and are brought up to date on what we are going to do, and why we are doing this, and where we will be doing this, and at the end of the lecture, although we are overwhelmed, we agree that we would do our best.

I have some free time, so I decide to stop at the Priaux Museum which has access to the genealogy of the island— exactly what I need to check up on my grandmother. The library at the Museum is used to doing this for visitors, so one of the librarians takes down all the data which I have brought with me. I make a date for later in the week.

I meet up with the rest of the group at noon, at the Grange Hotel, and have my first introduction to a Plowman's lunch. This is a fancy salad with bread, cheeses and tomatoes. We have no need for dessert. We leave to tour the rest of the Island. We go to Vale Castle, where you must navigate the tides carefully or you'll be stuck at the Castle until the tide turns again. We even go to visit the cricket field where we will begin "boring" our holes tomorrow. Dinner back at the hotel, our walk around the town afterwards, and then off to bed to worry about the next day.

WEDNESDAY, AUGUST 3

Thank goodness Bob is not a fanatic about time, and we have a leisurely breakfast and are ready in time to pile into the van with him and go to our site for the day. We go to a field next to a Boy Scout Encampment and retrieve our shovels, augurs, charts etc. from the car. I am assigned to keep the records of all the stuff we dig up. You start with a shovel to get through the first layer, and then you use the augur (looks like a HUGE screw driver) and bore down into the earth. You keep going down with the augur, bringing it up so you can see what you have uncovered, then put it back in the earth, and keep boring down until you reach water. With measurements, one has the depth of the land in that particular place. Then you go to another site, do the same procedure, and so on. The depths will be different in each location, and will allow the scientists to come to conclusions about how much land is lost or retained over a period of time.

We break for lunch, but first we have to shop for provisions... bread, cheese, cold cuts, sodas and chocolate bars. We get to the grocery store, but just then the clouds move in and the rain comes down. We cancel that plan and go next door to a restaurant where everyone has crowded in to get out of the weather, and so there is no room for us. We order take-out and go outside to sit on a concrete slab, under an umbrella, and eat our lunch. Earthwatch always warns that one must be adaptable at any time to a change in plans. We now have learned lesson No.1

The rain passes and we go back to work. This time we begin to name the layers of earth that show levels of times past and clues to what may have been going on then, which is recorded in the levels of the soil. Interesting speculations are brought forth. The easiest one to read is a charcoal colored layer, which indicates a fire— domestic, or a whole town, or a raging fire destroying much of the land.

Our day ends at 5 pm and we are taken back to our hotel, where we do chores and eat dinner in the hotel. No after-dinner walk this day because we have sore hands and backs. Destination— early bed— get ready to work!

SUNDAY, AUGUST 4

Today is a repeat of yesterday, but at least we have our lunch with us, so we start right in digging and drilling. We are having a good time with lots of laughter, snide remarks and getting to know our fellow men in this far off place where we are beginning to feel at home. We are also getting suntanned. The last team to dig here left part of their equipment at the bottom of the hole, so some of us had to go down and retrieve stuff. Our leader insists we are making headway, although some who go down the hole are beginning to wonder. As we work, we pick up extraneous information about Guernsey. There are shrews on the island, a few amphibians and other reptiles, but NO snakes. Birds abound, both land and sea species. The birds greet us each day when we arrive. Tomorrow will be our first free day and we are excited about going to the island of Sark.

MONDAY, AUGUST 5

I have been here before, but it is such an intriguing little island, I will be glad to see it again. This time, I notice that there are strange ledges built around all sides of the chimneys of the houses. I am enchanted to find out that these are for witches to rest upon, in case they are tired of flying around the area. The ledges provide sitting room and at the same time protect the houses from the witches flying down their chimneys and scaring the inhabitants. On the island, there are windmills and two schools. I also learn that the Dame of Sark— the island regent— still collects, as a feudal lord, a chicken for every person living in every household, every year, as payment of a sort of income tax to her.

We catch the early boat back to our island and go to visit the Victor Hugo house that sits high above the town, overlooking the harbor. Hugo lived here, in exile from France, for 16 years, and this is where he wrote his memorable *Les Miserables*. His house is filled with unusual and "exotic things" and is a museum to his own life. End of a long, but enjoyable day for our team.

TUESDAY, AUGUST 6

The next day, we survey certain areas for future work, which is great fun but a lot of walking, not up and down streets, but through backyards and vast meadows, filled with grazing cows. No one bothers us. At one spot in one meadow, we come across an old white bathtub and we try to guess why it is here. One of the team comes up with the answer—"Why of course it's a cow-wash!" We also are followed throughout our walk by a little orange and white cat, who seems to adopt us and we are reluctant to leave him, when we are ready to go.

We now start to survey one of the chosen areas. In the most basic of terms, surveying is the use of a tripod, on which is sitting a camera and a sort of binocular-eye piece through which one looks ahead to a numbered stake, which is being held by one of the team at a certain distance. The numbers on the stake record the height and the distance of the area being measured. Then you can back sight the survey to the tripod. It is really a leapfrogging art to attain the right measurements. Quite neat!

WEDNESDAY, AUGUST 7

Today is another gray, cloudy, misty and drizzly day but regardless we must work. So off we go the van. Interesting note (personal) is that I have always had a natural wave to my hair, but wow, this English weather is what I really need to put in a bottle... my hair is a mass of little curly ringlets due to the moisture in the air. This I find very agreeable because I don't have to do anything except run my fingers through it and it looks fine!

But back to our work. We are again drilling and digging and bringing up new and different signs of other soil relics to be recorded. Since we are adjacent to and not part of (sensible planning) the cricket field, we are joined by the island's cricket team for their matches. So those of us, who are not actively at work, can sit on the sidelines of the games and watch. It is similar to baseball but it is also very different. Different bats (mallets), different clothing (all white), different kind of bases, and slightly different scoring. What a grand opportunity for all of us. Later on that morning, we also do some surveying, but this time one has to stand on the beach— some of us in the water— and we make use of our "wellies" which we had been told to bring with us. Fortunately there are only little waves on this beach or else we might have been washed out to sea.

We retreat back to land and sit with our lunch in hand on a concrete slab, outside a pumping station. On Earthwatch expeditions, one has to be flexible, and so a concrete slab dining table is not an issue. By the end of the day, it has become really cold and clammy at the shore and we are glad to crowd into the van and head back to our quarters at the hotel. We warm up quickly, and then decide to go to an Indian restaurant for dinner. Superb food and we feel we deserve this treat.

THURSDAY, AUGUST 8

Tomorrow is our second and last day off, and we are heading for the island of Herm. On the boat, there are two cocker spaniels that entertain us with their charms.

Herm is a charming small island, next to Sark. It is basically a nature preserve on this island that is 1-1/2 mile long by 1/2 mile wide. There is one hotel, two pubs, a few cottages, two shops, a post office and two beach-stands for food. And there are puffins, and more puffins and then some more. One is not allowed to pick any flowers, one can't own a house, radios are not allowed on the beaches, and you have to wash your clothes between midnight and noon. In spite of these restrictions, Herm is becoming a resort. Sort of.

We're back on our boat to Guernsey after walking along all the dirt paths, having a nice lunch in the hotel, and taking many pictures of this wonderful little island and all its panoramic views. We arrive in time to see the German Occupation Museum on Guernsey, which is located in the Bourg where my ancestor Nicholas Tostevin lived.

Gosh, home ground for me!

Forgot to mention, that there was a sign on Herm, in front of one of the cottages that read, "Charlotte, our sow, gave birth to 9 piglets this a.m." Top that?

FRIDAY, AUGUST 9

This is our last day with the van, so we're in the van early and head for the Scout Fields to so some more mapping, leveling, and digging more holes. Then once more, over to the cricket field to await the arrival of the TV people, who arrive at three o'clock. They interview all of us and take lots of notes and of course, take lots of photographs. This makes all of us proud to have come on this expedition.

We go back to the hotel and have to clean out the van completely— scrub, rearrange it back to the way we found it when it was hired, polish, and clean it so it looks fine. It served us well.

SATURDAY, AUGUST 10

Before our work at the Museum, I go to the bakery to order a cake from us to "one of ours" who has a birthday today. Then over to the Museum where we finish up charts, graphs, and whatever else has to be done. I also stop by the library to pick up the genealogy work about my ties to Guernsey. They have taken it as far back as they can but stop when it becomes back-to-France, which they cannot do. I am delighted with all the names, etc. they find. I am now legally half French and half English.

We enjoy lunch this last day at the garden restaurant at the Museum. No one sees that we have brought our own lunch (made from scraps left in our refrigerator) because we have hidden our lunch bags under a hydrangea bush behind the building. But we do have a glass of wine, so we at least contributed something to the day's profit. As we meander back to the hotel, I pick up the birthday cake, stop in a shop to buy a lovely china Guernsey cow, and stop at the chandlery to pick up a Guernsey flag, which I have ordered. Everyone is doing their last minute shopping, sad chore, but necessary to be welcomed back home.

To start our last night celebration, we all attend a cocktail party in our room with food and drink set on the washing machine and the fridge— but no one seems bothered. Then off to a special seafood restaurant, where we all have fresh fish and tasty local wine, and the birthday boy loves his cake. We receive our Earthwatch shirts. Toasts are made. End of Guernsey scene.

SUNDAY AUGUST 11

The following morning we are all packed and waiting in the parlor of the hotel. A bus comes to get us and drives us to the airport. We say our final goodbyes and board our plane back to Heathrow. Great time, good people, interesting adventures, and wistful flight back to the States.

St. Peter's Port Harbor

We get our directions.

At work!

At work!

The augers.

Guernsey (Sark) resident.

Sark—The Seignor's house.

Chapter 7: After the Glaciers

CHAPTER 8

1992: INDONESIA (BALI)
SACRED BALI

INTRODUCTION

I knew nothing about this little island at the western tip of Indonesia. It sounded far away and exotic and a real adventure. The catalog gave me the specifics of the trip, the work planned and a chance to study something about Hinduism. I decided to sign up.

And then I had another idea. Part of my family lives on an island in the South China Sea, named Peng Chou, which is also part of Hong Kong. I could stop there with them for a few days, continue on through Singapore, and right over to Bali. Good!

MONDAY/ TUESDAY, JULY 13-14

Plans are made, Earthwatch accepts my application, and on a hot day in July 1991, I board a plane in Philadelphia and head for the Far East. A very long flight. Hong Kong is fun, but loud and noisy, with foreign smells, and many, many crowded streets. Then I am off to Singapore, which is quieter and more sedate. I take a driver and see what there is to see and eventually order a Singapore Sling at Raffles. The next day, I leave on Garuda Airlines for Bali.

WEDNESDAY, JULY 15

I arrive at Densaper Airport on Bali. After a visual startling ride through high clouds through which I see the tops of numerous mountains, some of which are volcanic. That's new! But when I deplane in Bali, I also see mountains. So I am ready. It is dark by now but there is the usual boy-with-a-sign and ELIZABETH is written on it so I follow him to a taxi. After an hour ride, I find myself at the gates of a long wall which I walk through. I am now on the property of a Mandala, here in the town of Obud, at which I will stay for the next two weeks.

A women escorts me to my quarters on the third floor of a house, which is more like a series of open porches, built one upon another with a central staircase. There is a wall around each porch but otherwise one is open to the sky. Quite a sight, and quite a nice feeling. Then I am taken immediately down the stairs and across the street to a shop that sells sarongs and has stayed open just for my arrival. I must have one of these wrap-around-skirts at once because we are leaving early in the morning and one must wear one of these pareoes (even the men) if we should chance upon a temple. I finally get to bed at a late hour and with the noise of the resident rooster, the barking of the resident dogs, and the roar of the residents' mopeds, I do not enjoy a restful night.

THURSDAY, JULY 16

A fitful night's sleep but am in time for breakfast down on the platform in the middle of this compound, surrounded by family dwellings, their own temple and many small shrines. Young boys are scrambling up and down the little trees, collecting flowers to be put at all the shrines in the compound, as they do each day. Today is a religious day so the town of Ubud is decorated with streamers, garlands, and ribbons of all kinds.

We are hurried onto our bus and driven to the Monkey Forest, where, of course, there are hundreds of monkeys including babies, hanging precariously around their mother's necks. Here is the Pula Dalam Temple, which is the first of many temples we are to visit—in our sarongs. A priest and a priestess are ringing bells and dispensing the holy water. The people arrive with baskets of food as offerings. Then, they take some of the holy water and incense; sit on their knees, and pray with their hands folded and their arms held skyward. The children are adorable and follow these rituals quietly and obediently. Before we leave, we go and look at a cemetery. Then back to our Mandala bungalow for lunch.

In the afternoon, we take a walk around Ubud. The Barong (a parade with music—Gamelon) is approaching and the dancing starts. The actual Barong is a mythical creature and a good one. Two children are dressed as this creature—one is the front and another is the back end. This is very funny. We soon go off to another temple where a story is being told by Balinese dancers with the long fingers that twist and curl, and next week we are to have a lesson in this art???

Then back again to Ubud, to sit on pillows and watch a man hold puppets behind a sheet, which is lit by small lamps and produces a weird picture, played and acted out vocally by the actors behind the sheet. We are allowed backstage for a few minutes to watch the musicians and the three puppeteers as they continue to work and tell the story.

Back for a late dinner and everyone goes right to bed, after our day of sightseeing.

FRIDAY, JULY 17

Have a little breakfast during which Ann Norton, our leader, reads the itinerary to us. There are a few minutes free so three of us walk into Obud to go to the post office and to exchange some money. On the way back, we meet Ann's assistant, Hans Guggenheim. He is a small, gentle, kind man who walks back with us. The bus is waiting and we pile in, and go to the "bathing spot", an archeological dig that was uncovered only 40 years ago. The bathing spot has three areas: 1— for lads and lassies, 2— for kings and queens, and 3— for husbands and wives. We go down into the forest to see an old Buddha, which has fallen into disrepair. Then onto a terrible lunch spot, where they didn't even have bread for sandwiches. Then back to the temple we visited yesterday where a priest is blessing a Barong (the parade of musicians and dancers). Splendid spectacle. The Barong moves out onto the street and we follow it for a while. This time we find a shrine, in the middle of a rice paddy. Then on to a town with a temple in the middle of a lily pond. We wade over to the temple, which has wonderful paintings on the ceiling about how life was before and after the Dutch came. Dr. Guggenheim and I talk together during the ride back to Ubud and decide that between us, we are puzzled by the fact that we are not learning anything here about Hindu Sacred Space, which is why we came. After dinner that night we go to see a local dance.

We do learn that the reason the Hindu shrines always have black and white checked tablecloths on their little altars is to represent good and evil, but they also look like the cloth shown at auto races back in the States.

SATURDAY, JULY 18

We are having a heavy rainstorm this morning, so all plans are cancelled to go to the Monkey Forest again, to meet another Earthwatch team. Everyone is going to sit around and talk all morning. Hans and I decide to go over to the Monkey Forest by ourselves, and meet a nice lady there, and also the monkeys who always are hanging around. At one point, one of the more aggressive monkeys tries to yank my backpack off and decides he would also like my camera. A guard nearby comes over and holds out food to the monkey who apparently thinks food is a better deal than my camera, and jumps off me. Hans and I walk into the nearby village and have a nice lunch, and then take a cab to the museum in town. On the way, I buy beautiful beads at one of the shops. I will bring them back home for a friend who makes jewelry. There is a rooftop tearoom at the museum and Hans and I cook up a scheme, whereby we WILL learn something about Hindu sacred places, and we will start tomorrow by hiring an interpreter. Like local folks, we get on a Bemo (bus) and ride back to Mandela where we are in time for dinner, and apparently no one missed us ????

SUNDAY, JULY 19

Hans and I walk into Ubud and go to meet the retired chief of the village where Pura Dalem temple is. Hans and I ask him questions, and the interpreter translates. There is a lot of cooperation and I write down some of stuff we learn.

Then back to Mandela. There is a celebration being held for the wife of the owner of the Mandela, at their own little temple in the complex. We have lunch, and then several of us begin to wonder out loud what we are doing here and why do we just go from one temple to the next, or attend festivals, or watch parades. I think the whole group is getting tired of all this sightseeing. We came a long way and paid a lot of money and we are not tourists. I forgot to mention that before we left, our "chief" took us to a cockfight, which was disgusting but as he explained, a serious part of the Hindu religion.

MONDAY, JULY 20

Today we drive to Kitamundi, the mountain temple grounds from which holy water for the entire island of Bali is sent forth. It channels down the mountain from Crater Lake, which is located just below the temple and then on through to other temples on Bali. Hans buys all of us big, fresh oranges that we devour. We drive past the Banyan tree temple and pull in to see if the Barong is still going on. No, but there's another cockfight. What else is happening is that the Temple is getting ready to welcome back from Java, their Temple God, and have laid out white carpets and a little gold chariot.

This God must be tiny. He doesn't come, and doesn't come, even though we wait for him. We wait so long, that we miss dinner when we finally get back. Thank goodness we had those oranges.

TUESDAY, JULY 21

We start the day by going to a production in a theater of the Barong. It is colorful, amusing, and well done. Take some pictures of a Buddist Temple next door. Then get in the bus to go to Senur. This is one of the beautiful beaches on the island, and here, the great sport is kite flying. It must be glorious when the beach is crowded with all those colors flying overhead. Today there are a few kites— enough for us to realize how spectacular they look. We have lunch at a seaside pavilion. Then we lounge for a while, and then walk up the street to get familiar with the town.

Next, we take the bus to another temple, built entirely of coral, and right on the edge of a huge cliff. However, since the temple is so wide open, the place is filled with monkeys, and there is no room for us. The view is spectacular. Across the water, in the distance, is Java and Indonesia. We watch and wait for the sunset but it is too cloudy for much color and so we get back on the bus and go back to Mandala for dinner. We have a birthday cake for one of the Earthwatchers.

It is now dawning on all of us that something has gone terribly awry in the planning of this Earthwatch trip. None of us can explain why we spend most days in the bus and continue to visit tourist spots and events, which are often exquisite sights, but WHAT ABOUT HINDU SACRED SPACE?

(Another tidbit picked up in our travels is that at the entrance to each compound or hutang-like dwelling, there is a sign, listing the father's name, the mother's name and the names of all the children. Very convenient!)

WEDNESDAY, JULY 22

Two girls from our team are to take lessons in Balinese dancing this morning. Several of the daughters of the owners of our Mandela are trained in this art and it is amazing to watch how they learn to curve their fingers, and twist their arms in this very sinuous way. We practice and practice and still continue to look like Americans who are trying to learn to do something they will never be able to do.

After the dance lesson, we board our bus and go to a nearby town to see a cremation. Death in this country is looked upon quite differently than that in the States. For one thing, the family has to deal with spirits (mostly bad ones) as well as the recently deceased one, and there are numerous customs that are peculiar (to us). Two huge wooden animals— a cow and a bull— have been decorated and will be the receptacles for the burning of the coffins. The animals have been picked up and moved by many men, being blessed by a very old priest, who sits cross-legged on a cushion and is carried toward the house in which the dead people had lived. Through the doorway to the house come family members with offerings, then two young people each in a small chair; then a line of mourners all covered by a long white sheet overhead, and then the coffins of the two deceased people, and then the whole group is moved over toward where the animals stand. The animals have meanwhile been sawed in half, so that now the coffins can be slid inside. Military flags, more offerings and flowers are then put inside the coffin, as well. The animal's doors are slammed shut, and kerosene is poured over each animal and lit. Huge flames shoot into the sky and the crowd watches as the scene is burned to the ground. We do not stay to see all of this— too long.

We return to our Mandela and after dinner, go to watch an artisan who makes his living designing masks. Hans and I have invited our interpreter friend to join us, so we have an excellent lesson in this art.

THURSDAY, JULY 23

Hans and I leave at 9 a.m. and go to the chief's house with our interpreter. We talk to the chief for over an hour about the soul and other aspects of the Hindu religion. Then he takes us up to the Monkey Forest where we are the only ones allowed inside the temple. We stay for several hours and learn all the different places and the different reasons for their existence. Now the purpose for our trip to Bali begins to unravel for us. I am so glad we have gone ahead on our own, but I don't think our other leader would be as enthusiastic about our secret.

Hans and I go back to the main street in Ubud and have some lunch. Then we walk down the Monkey Forest Road, stopping in shops and walking in back alleys of the town, absorbing the sight, seeing the differences in some of the neighborhoods and watching the average person doing what average people do all over the world. We stop at a neighborhood produce stand and buy fruit to take back to Mandela. After a nice dinner, we all meet on Ann's porch and listen to the plans for the rest of our stay. We ask questions about our project and she gives us answers that really aren't answers. We just think, "She doesn't get it".

FRIDAY, JULY 24

We get up a bit later than usual and the group goes off shopping. I decide not to go because I want to get my notes organized and I feel good after I do this.

I go down and walk slowly through the entire compound. I find the temple and study if for a while, and then go on to see all the little offerings that are left in the doorways of the residents each and every morning. I find where the roosters live (and secretly plan their demise), where the resident dogs sleep–right beneath the floor on which I live, and where the vegetable gardens and flower gardens are. It is a very well established neighborhood right inside these stonewalls. And there is a certain air of peacefulness, quiet and reverence here which I find very nice.

Hans appears and we both agree to go and find our interpreter's house. On the way, we see another cremation. This one is not so elaborate–a different class of being, we suppose. Down the road, we find three teenage boys with their cock-fighting birds in their front yard. One of the boys lets me stroke his bird, which is a stately male. I can't imagine owning such a beautiful bird and letting him engage in a cockfight. We sit and talk (through our interpreter of course) and hear him tell a bit of his life. We are thrilled to be where we are.

When we leave, we continue to wander in and out of shops to see if I can find a carved monkey. (I collect an animal from each trip I take to remind me of the places I have been). No monkeys!! After dinner

---

Chapter 8: Sacred Bali

that night we all retire to our rooms, and I hear a noise from the garden below. I look, and it is Hans with a package, which he tosses up to me. I unwrap this strangely shaped package and there is a little wooden carved monkey! Hans never told me where he found it, but I know he didn't carve it himself.

SATURDAY, JULY 25

Starts out to be a regular day with plans to see another puppet show; but news arrives that there is a huge fair going on in the town at the largest Temple. Of course we have to go. It is quite spectacular. The temple is completely decorated in white and yellow and looks like a big spring flower. Everyone is there.

We sit around for some time, talk and take pictures— all the time waiting for the show that never happens.

Back to Mandela for a quick lunch and then we hurry back into town to see the show, after all. Wrong! We do sit on the platform with the gamelon musicians and Hans sketches the sights. We give up again and take our bus and go to Kitatami to see "Trances". This is a new word in our vocabulary. Now, we go to a rural town where there are paintings on the ceiling. Not half as elegant as our temple in Ubud. There is a parade of offerings, some flags and then large boxes covered with cloth and carried on bamboo platforms by men who keep running into one another. We don't mean to be unholy, but it certainly does look funny and we giggle.

Apparently, the men get "manic" (almost transformed) into trances. None of us quite understand the whole process or meaning but it is mesmerizing. We stay late, all the time watching this peculiar ceremony, and then we are all late for dinner. We eat what is available, and have to go pack because tomorrow, we are to get up before dawn.

SUNDAY JULY 26

We have to get up REALLY, REALLY early to be on the bus by 5 a.m. to drive through the dark hours to the airport. We board our flight to Yokyakarta in Indonesia, which is only an hour away, but they do feed us breakfast. As we fly over Java, we see some of the high volcanic mountains and one is smoking. I am glad when we pass that one as I can imagine a worse scenario. After we land, we are taken to a nearby Holiday Inn and leave our luggage. It is only 7:30 am and we are on our bus headed to Borobudor, which is the largest Buddist monument in the world. It is VERY large. It is not a monastery because no one lives there. To climb the whole monument one takes "aisles" that go round and round and up and up to the top. It is hot and our pace slows, and we lose the voice of our guide. We figure we can catch up with the rest of the tour talk later on, and after 1-1/2 hours, some of us decide to retreat or simply to head down to the bottom. We wait, and then all of us have lunch at Borobudor since we are very hungry and very tired. Back to our hotel by mid-afternoon, in time to wash up and dress carefully because we are to be guests at an Indonesian Princess's home. Palace?

We enter a large hall that has a stage at one end, and we are seated to watch a performance of Javanese dancers— the ones with the long arms and sinuous fingers.

Meanwhile, tables are set behind us, and we are even offered a drink with cloves in it, and bananas as hors d'oeurves. The dinner is delightful but there is little conversation because we are more interested in looking around at the artwork in the hall than we are in our usual chit-chat. The silence eventually becomes a little boring, so we are glad when we are ushered back to our seats in front of the stage. More dancing goes on, and even a little story, kind of dance that we can understand. Lots of photos and clapping, and then the Princess appears (found out she is Princess Ratu Amnom and this is her "house"). She thanks us and we thank her, and then we are off to the bus, our hotel, and we are all mighty tired.

MONDAY, JULY 27

Up at 4:45 a.m. to get an early start to Brobobudor because one of our groups is going to do a video of us before the crowds appear. Hans and I break off and go to the Museum to search out the good/evil pictures of buried panels of Brobobudor that are only in this place. The curator of these panels in not in, so we leave and go back to the monument and on up to the "first aisle" to revisit some of these panels. Hans does some rubbings of the panels.

We go back again to the Museum and find someone else to answer our questions. This is some sort of game we seem to be playing. I become the errand girl between the Earthwatch group and the museum group. Eventually we all agree to meet at the bus in one hour. Once again, things get all mixed up (Earthwatch guide line: Be ready for change in plans!—seems appropriate right here). We all do get back to the hotel and we're fine. After dinner, the curator does show up (!!!!) and has videos for us. Meanwhile, someone from the group has turned her ankle while on a shopping spree in the afternoon, so Hans accompanies her to a local doctor who straps her ankle and gives her pills.

We go to bed early because we have another EARLY rising the next morning.

TUESDAY, JULY 28

Up at 5:30 a.m. this morning, a quick breakfast and onto the bus by 7 a.m. Off to the airport and after much confusion (what else is new?), we are led to the correct plane and take off to return to Bali.

When we land, a jitney is waiting for us to take us to the Gazebo Hotel. Some of us just sit on the veranda, looking out on the beach and ocean. It is lovely to just SIT in one place, with no apparent deadlines. Eventually, we all have lunch in the restaurant on the beach and get into the weirdest discussion about skulls and skeletons. You would think we are planning a Halloween party. Hans wants to leave his skull to science. I tell him that at the rate we are going, here in Bali, he may have to leave more.

The two leaders, Ann and Hans, leave first to get their flight back to the States. Those of us who have time to waste will be taking a cab to the airport. So we sit around wondering what the conversation must be like between Ann and Hans. We will have to wait until we all get back to the states to hear. If we do, hear, that is— maybe not.

The rest of us leave Bali after a real mess trying to change Bali currency into American currency, but we manage. We leave the beautiful little island with mixed emotions about what we learned and how different it was from our expectations.

EPILOGUE

Several weeks after our return from Bali, I received a letter from the President of Earthwatch, apologizing for the lack of following the curriculum as spelled out in the catalog. He had met with the leader

Ann, and her assistant, Hans. Ann was not to continue with Earthwatch adventures again, and Hans was excused from not following protocol, but he could not be faulted for using his own ingenuity to find some of the answers we were all seeking

Hans and I kept up a correspondence for several years, but by then he was off to many new places and I lost track of him. But he certainly made a good trip for all of us— one way or another.

Bas Relief

Bas Relief

Bas Relief

Bas Relief

Hans drawing.

Author's rendition of Bali gods.

CHAPTER 9

1993: RUSSIA (MOSCOW)
EXCAVATION AT RED SQUARE

INTRODUCTION

Archeology in Moscow started in the 1920's but it did not become a full-scale operation until after the last war. Architects and archeologists created a special Department of Preservation of Historical Monuments to work closely with other committees dedicated to the same cause. As volunteers, we will begin to excavate sites linked with events of Moscow's history. We will collect and analyze artifacts, which will tell much about the material culture of the past. There are hopes of finding remnants of the original kremlins (wooden, enclosed communities) beneath part of the city where they are believed to have been built. We will be looking for vestiges of charred wooden houses, walls and streets and pavements, as well as glass, pottery, metals, tiles, jewelry and religious objects. The occupational layers of soils here in Moscow seem to have preserved many of these artifacts; in fact there seem to be more available pieces of information available here than in many other European cities.

And so here we are, ready and willing, and we hope we are able to carry out our task.

SATURDAY, JULY 31

Friends drive me to my Philadelphia Airport, and I am very nervous about this trip because they have told me that when I arrive in Moscow, there will be lots of cabs waiting for me, and most of them will be "'gypsy" cabs that will gladly offer you a ride, and then take you into a neighboring forest, and do bad things (like kill you for your money) and never take you to the city. I love people who say such things, and then I have to get on the plane and worry, worry, worry. I do this, but nothing goes awry, and in Zurich, I easily transfer, and am off to Russia.

SUNDAY, AUGUST 1

I must admit that when I deplane in Moscow, I run straight to Intourist and ask them for a driver and a private car. In 15 minutes, I am in a van with a nice driver (I hope). It takes 25 minutes to drive to my hotel, which is on the outside ring road around Moscow, and is known as the Hotel for Retired Russian Generals. That sounds imposing, and I am not disappointed. There is a circular drive and a rather stately entrance, and immediately after stepping into the lobby, I am greeted by the Earthwatch leader, Nicole Logan and the rest of Team 1, for the archeological dig, here. We are assigned to our rooms– my own room with another room adjoining, and a bathroom in between. The shower will be only COLD. No hot water, yet. We are too late for dinner, so go upstairs where Nicole has ordered sandwiches and tea for us. We chatter a bit, and then everyone, suffering sleep depravation, goes to his/her room and goes right to bed.

MONDAY, AUGUST 2

We all go down to the cafeteria in the hotel for breakfast. I must admit that we stood and gaped at the table before we sat down. 1) No jelly; only caviar 2) small bottle of vodka at each place, and otherwise regular breakfast. We have our own long table in a separate room, which makes it difficult for us to see the "retired generals". Well, maybe later.

We then take our bus and go to see the "site" where we are to be digging, etc. for the next two weeks. It is right in the middle of the city. We are in Manewzhaya Square (that's Menage in English) across the street from the Kremlin, at the foot of a ramp up to Red Square. There are nine holes dug up already, and there are three of these pits that are waiting for our excavating work. The Russians are so poor, that they only have a few ladders, and so they have made ladders out of wire, for our use. I go down one pit, on one of these ladders, and when I come up, I plead with Nicole (by now, our leader, whom we have been asked to call by her first name) to let me stay above ground. I have a "trick" knee, which I know would trick me right out of commission on one of those ladders. So, when we are asked our choices of work, here on Menage Square, I choose to wash, classify, and put together as many of the shards as I can, which are brought to me. Others, dig, sieve, remove dirt to a common pile, etc. etc. I am thrilled. I gather concrete blocks and put them together to make a workbench of sorts, and begin to sort out this HUGE jigsaw puzzle of relics. What a great time. I am seated next to the fence (the site is all fenced in) where people gather and ask question. It is like being on stage. Sometimes, other workers get bored being so far down in the pits, and come up, and help me for a while. Some stay for hours. We "restored" bottles from Lithuania and Latvia, bowls from our own area of Moscow, pots, dishes, parts of jewelry (we think), coins, buttons, etc. In the pits, they uncover wooden sidewalks; aquaducts over the river that flows there, the bricks and mortar of buildings, and all manner of smaller treasures.

Nicole takes us around the corner to the Metropole Hotel to get our money changed. We are looking at the Bolshoi Theater to our right. The Metropole is so besieged by tourists, that a bus has been hired and turned into a currency exchange to help with the crowds. We also buy bottled water, which we learn is more expensive than vodka. There is plenty of both being sold.

Then on to our tour of the city. We see Gorky Park across the river (Neva) and have a lovely view of the Kremlin from there, with the gold onions on the steeples of the many churches inside the Kremlin walls. We see the Olympic Stadium, and then we must hurry back to our hotel since the head of the Archeological Office is presiding at a dinner for us at the Paradise Restaurant, which sounded very un-Russian, but was very elegant. We also are introduced to the fact that vodka is consumed at a rapid rate at every dinner. One has to be demure and refuse toast after toast, or one will not remember anything by the time the celebration is over.

Moscow is quite a grand city and we were impressed by a certain atmosphere of dignity that pervades throughout– it has a good deal of ambiance.

TUESDAY, AUGUST 3

Everyone is up on time, but I bet most of us are not feeling too spry. At 9 am, we go directly to the site, and work begins. I am busy piecing together whatever I can find that remotely looks like something else. Not like a jigsaw puzzle, where you usually start with the edges; no, here there is no edge. It's color, shape, and form that matters. And then the glue. We are provided with homemade glue (looks like flour mixed with water, to me), which doesn't hold the way it should. So at lunchtime, I run quickly up onto Red Square, where the department store GUM is located, and find a store inside with glue on one counter. I buy a few tubes of it, and race back before anyone misses me. That afternoon I use it on some shards until one of the project professors sees me and says "No, you can't use that stuff; it will harm the natural materials, eventually" and grabs the tubes, and I have to go back to Russian glue, after all. I never did find out the "why" about the glue, and someday will ask an archeologist if this is so. I also leave my position by the fence to go over to the Moskova hotel, across the street, where the nearest bathroom can be used. A guard grabs me and frisks me, but he does appropriate my camera, until I am through.

We have our usual lunch, at noon, which is bread, cheese, salami, cookies, and warm orange soda. At 3 pm, as promised, we go up to Red Square, and are given a history lesson of that which we are seeing now. Then we take our bus and drive down a crowded street to see the Lubyianka, a large yellow building that looks scary because of the awful treatment given the prisoners there, and we avert our eyes, after one peek. Next is the City Museum of Moscow, which already has many relics in its collection of early Russia. We are all getting tired so insist we must return to our hotel in order to get ready for dinner. And so we return after a trolley ride, a bus ride, and then a long walk through a park to the hotel. After dinner, there is very little enthusiasm for chatter, and early to bed.

Most of the birds I am seeing are as large as crows but are dark gray and/or black. I find out they are ravens. They also hang out at the site and every morning, we see them sorting through our garbage (lunch) from the previous day. Salami rinds, and bread crusts? Whatever.

WEDNESDAY, AUGUST 4

At least, on this trip, we do not have to get up at the earliest of hours. Since we are working in the center of the city, it is useless to start before 9:00 am because none of the Moscovites on the dig arrive before then. Another day of playing with the pieces. It is fun to be interrupted by visitors (through the fence) who want to understand just what and why we are doing this. Sure breaks up the hours to play teacher to those who are new to this profession.

After lunch, we take off on a long walk to the other side of the Kremlin wall and in through a door and into a small Kremlin museum in the basement of one of the churches. These little rooms contain very early remains found in this Church of the Assumption, when it was built. Outside the church, the golden onion-shaped steeple is splendid in the bright sunlight. Next, is the Armory Museum, also one of grandeur. The display here is of jeweled books, goblets, chalices, urns and plates—in gold and silver encrusted with jewels. Most of them were made right here in the Kremlin, in the tsar's workshop. One begins to understand the power and the wealth behind this great country, although our most familiar pictures are of poor peasants and their lowly existences in a lowly countryside. Also, we see ornate carriages, a room full of horse adornments, fabulous dresses, and polished armor. This city had, what we would call, some real panache! And of course we have to stop in the delightful museum shop, where we ladies could have spent the afternoon. But no!

Back to work for a while and then dinner at our hotel. A few of us leave to go to the Circus and there are the trained bears, dancing and tumbling. One day, we actually see a man in the park, walking a bear cub on a leash, and we wonder if the bear is being brought up to be a performer in the circus. We don't know enough Russian language to ask him. What a good evening.

(Find that the gold carriages were made in France!)

THURSDAY, AUGUST 5

Off again, at the usual time, to our usual spot. Sometimes, a few of the Earthwatchers manage the Moscow subway, first to see if they can find their way, and secondly, to get a look at the artful decor in most of the stations. There are crystal chandeliers, lots of paintings, and sculpture, but also smaller pieces of art, as friezes, and moldings– which make it very pleasant to view, even if you're on your way to a dull job.

We work hard during the morning, and then a very attractive news photographer appears on our scene to take pictures of these western volunteers who are digging around their city. We have gotten publicity through the Archeological Society and have been on the radio and TV stations. But this is the first time we will have appeared in print. Now we feel like we really matter.

During lunch, I grab my sandwich and rush through GUM because someone has told me about a good art store around the corner. I buy a wonderful Russian type bear, a nice Russian bird, and two egg baskets. Robert tells me later I have bought two lettuce washers. Oh, well, who will know? I'm back in time at the site to attend two lectures under the tent, where we go if it rains. They are good, and then it really does start to rain, so some of us go back to our hotel because a visit to a museum has been cancelled. We do chores, have dinner, and go to Ada and Leonid's apartment. (Ada is Nicole's advisor and often accompanies us, and Leonid is an architect, in charge of restoration in the city.) We see slides of previous archeological finds in Moscow, shown by Dr. Veckler, who is the head of the whole Archeological Department in the city.

I must describe their apartment, which is a very nice for apartments in Moscow. First it is very small, with their bathroom out in the corridor at the end of the hallway! There are bookshelves, and piles of books all over. There are lace curtains and little lamps with red paper shades. We sit on heavy Russian style furniture and are served coffee and tea from an elaborate silver urn and gorgeous plates filled with tiny cakes of wonderful flavors. We feel as though we are "in a Russian novel" and wish we had not worn our American clothes. What a delightful moment. We then are served brandy from tiny silver cups, and now we are sure we have become truly Russianized.

FRIDAY, AUGUST 6

After my now usual routine of bringing coffee back to my room, I get organized for the day, get into my work clothes and go off in our car to the site. Work on the shards of pottery, with some new additions that have other countries' name on them. This apparently proves that Russia was already trading with Britain and the Baltic countries. Most of these seem to be bottles of liquor. Wow, even that long ago, since Vodka seemed to be the current choice. During our 10 minute break at 11 a.m., I dash up to Red 'Square, and go over to the church where our friend Leonid is the architect in charge in of the restoration. Outside the church there is a little kiosk that is staffed by two ladies who sell "things" to help the finances of the church. I quickly buy two trinkets, tiny but carefully painted in rich colors. Then a run down the hill to the site and when I show my treasures to the rest of the team, they all want them. Nicole excuses them to go back to the church I found and apparently they buy out the entire inventory that is available. Makes us feel good to have spent the rubles.

After lunch, we have another tent lecture, and this time they have removed the tent to a quieter part of the site; we have had trouble hearing some of the former lectures due the city noises at the original spot. We finish our chores for the day, and go over to the Metropole Hotel to exchange money. As I pass through the lobby, I spy a perfectly beautiful carving of St. Basil's church, which is on Red Square, one of the most visited and photographed sight in Russia. I buy it, even though it is expensive and today, as I write this, it is still on my desk, here at home.

We return to the site for our afternoon visit to another "must see" on Nicole's list. She is determined that we will see everything that is important to Moscow/Russia while we are here. Such a good leader, she is. We are headed to a museum, but it is small one and we get lost. Since none of us have any idea of where we are anyway, it doesn't much matter to us and instead, we end up in the studio of a well-known artist– Mr. Vasnetsov– whose pictures are somewhat grisly, but occasionally there is one that looks a bit like a Wyeth. What a gamut of talent. His house is charming and made out of pink (!) logs.

We choose to walk back to the hotel, and go through some blocks of typical drab apartment houses, but it is through a park and that is a nice change.

After dinner, a vendor comes to our hotel, and his wares are so meager, that we all feel sorry for him and buy everything he has. Well, almost. Today is our spending day apparently, and we all sleep well with good consciences.

SATURDAY, AUGUST 7

We all have breakfast together but then split up to do our own thing, on our first free day! Four of us take two busses to the convent at Novodevichy, out at the back of nowhere. We can't believe we get here by ourselves. We first visit the church and then the museum. The church has floor-to-ceiling icons (religious paintings). There is a screen that the congregation and the priests call iconostasis. It is very ornate and very beautiful. No ladies are allowed behind the screen. One did, at one time, and was struck mute for 20 years. We all buy a picture of the icons because they are so unusual. Then we go next door to the cemetery where a number of famous people are buried. The graves are well cared for; there are fake flowers on many of them and even photographs of the deceased, on others. Stalin's wife is there (Svetlana), Krushchev (a strange headstone of black and white marble which is cut into a window), Stanislavsky, Scriabin,

Prokofiev, Gogol, Shostakovitch and lots more we are unfamiliar with. We move on to the Tretyakev Museum, which is famous for its collection of icons. Here is the famous painting of Ivan the Terrible, who killed his son; but today it is "out" being restored. Too bad– this is one of the "must" on the tourist tour. I am surprised that many of the icons are painted on simple pieces of wood. I wonder why this kind of art never caught on in our country. It is so much less expensive than a canvas.

In a cab we go back to the center of the city and as we cross the river, we are treated with a marvelous picture of the Kremlin and the office building where Yeltsin has his offices. Then on to the Pushkin Museum, which is another "must" and here we encounter a long line of people waiting to get in. The reason is the Matisse show, which recently closed in the States and is now here. Several of us have seen that show, so we move on to Arbat Street, which is the craft, souvenirs, some good art and "whatever you choose" street. Some of us eat, and others browse.

We return to the hotel and dress up for dinner at a famous restaurant known for its intelligencia of the Russian arts. (Who chose this for us?). Anyway, I must describe the place. Long tables with champagne, vodka, water, and beer at EACH place. Tons of food— salads, spiced meats, fish, caviar, blini with sour cream, individual soup tureens, meat, potatoes and carrots; then ice cream and coffee. How do you walk after that presentation?

But what a day we all have had. No trouble going to sleep, for any of us.

INSERT FOR AUGUST 7

Several of us take pictures inside a bus in which we are riding. On the dashboard of the bus, the driver has a small bouquet of lovely homegrown flowers and all in an old Pepsi Cola can.

Russian parents always have their arms around their children, when out walking. And they lean over and hug them, at least once every block. It makes us wonder if there is much child abuse here.

All the cars in this city are small. The only time one would see a normal or large sized car is when a dignitary is riding inside. The cars owned by the people are not only dented and out of shape, but nothing seems to work correctly. On our trip to the airport, when the project is over, it is raining hard and the windshield wipers don't work more than one swipe across, so the driver has to get out and give them a push. It finally gets too much for him, and he grabs a stick, leaves the door open and pokes around the door and hit the wipers again and again. Makes for a nice ride for us in the back seat!

The traditions of the wedding ceremonies are certainly different here. After the church ceremony, the bride and groom get into their car, with two other people, and drive around the city to lay flowers on the graves or monuments of important people. They can't afford more than one car, so the rest of the family and friends wait for them back in the reception hall. One car that stops across from our dig has two huge bows tied to the front of the roof of the car, and a huge fake wedding ring also tied to the top of the car. The four people, from the car, pray at the statue in front of the Kremlin wall, then, jump back in the car, and apparently drive to the next monument.

"Eez-bah" is the name of the very ornately decorated farmhouses seen as one drives out in the country from the city. Dachas are the country homes, which are near the sea, and owned by the wealthy people.

One touching scene on our drive is seeing an old man and a woman, sitting on separate stools, and tending to their goats, in the meadow.

Buses have curtains, about 12 inches deep, hanging over all the windows.

SUNDAY, AUGUST 8

Today we have a bus to take us on an all-day trip, out of Moscow, and north to Zagorst. This is where the Orthodox Russian church started and it is the most sacred and most revered place in all of Russia.

On the way, we see the Space Rocket monument to hail the first of the Russian journeys into outer space. Nearby is also a gigantic statue dedicated to the Russian men and women who are depicted as running forth with hammer and sickle. It was on display at the World Exhibition in Paris in 1937. "Workers and Women-Collective Farmers". It is very impressive.

Then on to Zagorst, past big forests with many birch trees (favorite tree in Russia). The countryside is lavish, with yellow and lavender flowers. The city of Zagorst is filled with churches with domes of different colors. We pass a hospital, a holy-water font, and there are lots of people. We have to wear a skirt when we go to the monastery. As usual, we have a Russian guide, so Ada is along to translate for us. It takes a very long time to do all the translation because Russians love to talk. And then more.

When we reach the monastery, we are "let loose" on our own, and some of us find a spot to sit on the front steps. Apparently the "brothers" (priests) are gathering inside, so no one is allowed to go in. Soon the doors open and the "Trainees" come out, in a parade fashion. They are dressed in long black robes but with different kinds of hats; some caps, some mitres, and some like small stovepipes. At the end of the procession, the priests finally emerge. They must be the priests of priests, in long black robes, tall hats, and beards on chins. A women, standing on the side of the walkway, drops to her feet and reaches out to touch the robe of one of the high priests, and he flings his left hand to her and she kisses it. I am astounded at this overt show of faith. The monks and the priest disappear from view. Now we are able to go into the church and marvel at its beauty.

Boris Godunov and his family are buried in the churchyard.

We stop next in a National Park to have lunch. We have forgotten to bring cups for our soda. Did you ever try sipping from a big bottle of soda, upside down so that you don't contaminate the drink for others? I do. I am covered with orange soda for the ride back to Moscow.

But here, in this park is a famous house named Abramtsevo. It was a retreat for writers, musicians, painters and other members of the arts. It is well attended each summer and Gogol mentions it in his books. There is a charming little fairy-book church in the woods behind the house, and a children's playhouse nearby. Another building on the property was used as a hospital, during one war.

During the long ride back to Moscow, our guide points out some more important churches and houses (one house where the founder of Zagorst lived), but our eyes are closing. We have been "churched out" and our hotel looks very good to us when we arrive.

MONDAY, AUGUST 9

We are back to work today after our wonderful weekend, in and out of the city, but wherever, it was a grand experience.

Two more people come up from the "pits" and want to work with me on connecting the pieces of pottery, glass, and a miscellaneous pile of "what's this". We have a good time in spite of having this watery Russian glue. When our newcomers complain that we could stick stuff together with the glue from GUM, we inform him that we have tried, but we were told it is not allowed. So "when in Rome..." and we continue as we have been doing.

At lunchtime, I eat and then excuse myself to run over to the Metropole Hotel to change some money. On the first block, I pass stairs going down to the subway and notice a woman sitting on the steps, with a baby in her lap. There are three younger children playing on the steps near her. The next thing I know, the three kids race to me and try to rip my fanny-pack off my body. They are clever little pests and one I am able to subdue when I knee him in the groin. The other two are constantly on the attack and just as I am beginning to tire and think I will lose this battle, there is a screech of brakes, and a car pulls up to the curb and a man in uniform jumps and heads for the kids. It is a Kremlin guard, and he must be used to this kind of scene. God bless! He chases the kids down the block, comes back to see if I am okay (I am), and I continue on my way and he goes after the kids' mother and the baby. I don't hang around to see what else happens.

When I get back to the site, I am told I have missed all the excitement. When they tell me, I fill in the whole group, and the part I play in the drama, and they are astounded that I am not injured. "Just another day in Moscow", I assure them and go back to the shards and pieces of pottery.

That night, after dinner at the hotel, we go to Ada's and Leonid's again, and see more slides and pictures of Moscow archeology, and enjoy coffee from the urn and treats from the pretty china.

A long day.

TUESDAY, AUGUST 10

Another day at the office! Oops, I mean the site. We all work energetically and happily and get a number of pitchers, bottles, and two cups and find a spoon.

After lunch, several of us run up to Red Square to see Lenin's tomb. We have been watching all morning to see when there is the shortest line. The tomb is open today to the public and we have to dodge around the tourists. We think we are so smart, but the Kremlin guards stop us as we "dodge" around, and we decide we better wait until a better day. On the way back to the site, we absolutely have to stop in GUM to see what kind of clothes they offer. There is a Lafayette's French department store and we are amazed at the similarity of the fashions here. Very much U.S.A. it turns out to be. The prices are a bit higher, however.

Now we work until 3 p.m., and then go off to see the Moscow Department of Architecture. We see a huge map of Moscow with little "monopoly" houses and buildings. Also see another map of "Moscow Tomorrow". Amazing. There is a video of us Earthwatchers digging away in the pits, sifting the dirt, photographing all aspects of the site, and an engaging (of course) several moments of the puzzle solvers or the glue group.

We go to the hotel for dinner, and an early night to bed.

P.S. After my run-in with the gypsies (both Mother and children) I take a close look at the uniforms in the city. Policemen wear uniforms and high boots and look like Storm Troopers, particularly those in charge of security around Lenin's Tomb. Traffic cops wear light blue shirts; and Army men wear khakis, as in our hotel.

WEDNESDAY, AUGUST 11

We have our regular routine at the site until 10:30 a.m. and then hustle off to see the churches inside the Kremlin walls. This is a rare opportunity that Ada and Nicole have arranged for us– a privileged visit. Our first stop is at the Church of the Assumption with its five-gilded domes where the coronations of Tsars and Emperors took place. Then there is the Church of the Archangel Michael next door, the Church of the 12 Apostles, and several others, which I can't remember, and didn't write down, in time. So within the walls are the great churches of the country and they are mighty looking, to be sure. One smaller church is for the Patriarch of the Russian religion, and there is a little window above the sanctuary in the room where he stayed, and through this window he could hear when the service was starting, and go running down the stairs, to be on time. The church has two lovely entrance columns– one of blue and one of gold. Stunning.

We come back to earth (literally), and return to work at the site until 5:00 pm. Then over to Dr. Vecklers house (he is the head of all the archeology here) for a worker's party. It is a hearty meal with of course, lots of beer and vodka, and everyone toasts each other, and when we are all fed and toasted, we are shown the laboratories across the street where the fine-tuning of the finds and the delicate work is carefully and slowly finished. (Now I find out why we weren't allowed to use USA glue. Too harsh?)

When the party is over, the young Russian friends of ours, now, invite some of our crew's younger members to go to a pub (or whatever they call it), so they do, and the rest of us head back to the hotel and a good night's sleep.

THURSDAY, AUGUST 12

When we get to the site we notice that something is happening up on Red Square. Of course we can't contain our curiosity, so a few of us sneak out and up the road onto the square. Wow! Lenin's Tomb is open today to the public. The last time this happened we didn't have enough time to stand in line. This time, we decide to stay and wait, and take the consequences. So we line up. There are very stern looking guards, standing in their full-regalia uniforms with the high boots, which scare me to even look at. And when they walk from one station to the next, they goose-step.

The line moves quickly because I think everyone else besides me is terrified of annoying these guards. As a result, we enter the tomb and go down the steps into the viewing room in about 1/2 hour. I am amazed at two things about Lenin– one, is that he was quite short (why do I always think important people need to be tall), and number two that he had red hair (and it is still fiery red) and it is totally uncombed. I realize that these qualities are not what I should be thinking about, so I don't voice them. Just say that I am impressed. But the line is gently but firmly led out of the room, and that was that. (I will say that Lenin looked much better than Mao did when I saw him in Tiananmen Square in Bejing). Outside, under cover by the Kremlin wall are the graves of several other important Russians, including Stalin, who we all thought had been moved elsewhere.

We return to the Site, and work diligently for the rest of the day, hoping to make up for our "excursion" It was never mentioned.

We have a host of tourists in the P.M. who, this time stand and talk for some time. The most outspoken are two young men from Israel. One of them hands me a piece of broken tile. I have no idea from whence it came, so I accept it, he thinks, as one of ours. When he leaves, I put it in my pocket. We don't want any non-Russian relic in our splendid collection!!!

At lunch I scurry off to a new art store, and buy a doll and a tiny painting. On the way back to the site, I see some more gypsies and give them the 4-finger gypsy sign for evil, and they flee. I feel empowered.

At 3 p.m. we are off to the Romanov House, which is a fine residence and we have a delightful tour of this wooden house. The Romanov who lived here was the father of the first Romanov Tsar. One is a tsar if the kingdom is large enough; otherwise you are only a king!

After dinner that night and late packing, some of us gather in one of the rooms and talk about the trip, as a whole. I start with a positive reaction to everything that has transpired, except being mugged, but that adds some thrill to the story. I am surprised that there are a number of complaints of not meeting our '"needs" or our "wants". No one got sick, no one got hurt, no one got lost, and certainly no one was bored.

FRIDAY, AUGUST 13

We are all perked up for this day. We all behave when we are called and arrive at the site early, because the American Ambassador is coming to visit. We have worn clean clothes, and spent a bit of time learning "political correctness" in our speech and in our language. We clean everything in sight, and clear away that which we deem to be unsightly. He arrives on time, in a grand black car with American flags stuck on each front fender. His wife accompanies him and a 12-year-old girl name Victoria, whose father is outside our site, working on new pavement. The Ambassador had asked her if she would like to come with them to see what it was like inside the fence. The little girl is sweet, and smiles often, but offers no advice or encouragement of speech. (We all wonder how she explained her adventure to her parents when she got home). The Ambassador takes his time and looks down into all the pits, and scrutinizes the pottery, etc. display, over in my corner. If he had touched one of "my" pieces, I might have had to slap his hand. And I would be in the Lubiyanka in a second. They are very gracious, and Dr. Veckler (who has come to the site, also) and Nicole make sure he sees the entire area, and of course he is overwhelmed at all that has been accomplished, and when he leaves, there are many gracious thanks and good wishes and then we all go back to work.

Lunch has been delayed but we finally eat, and then go back to work, not to unclean our spots, but to put away and clean our tools, and leave the site.

Several of us go back to the Pushkin Museum, which we had bypassed several days ago, and had felt shameful for not waiting in line, like everyone else did. We get there and walk right in because there is no line. We go to see all the exhibits except the Matisse, which of course we had seen back home in the U.S. It is worth the return.

Back to the hotel in a cab and on the way, count 27 cars broken down on the road, and an accident by the side of the road with a body, covered with burlap, lying in the grass. This sobers us up, even though we have had nothing to drink, and we are glad to have something pleasant to look forward to in the evening.

It is our farewell dinner, down in our dining room. We are served an elaborate spread of a wide range of meat, potatoes, vegetables, fruits, caviar, relishes, side dishes (which I don't recognize, but eat anyway) and an incredible amount of drinks– vodka, beer, water, juice and then cakes and puddings, and coffee, coffee, coffee, while the endless toasts were proposed. I even get up and toast our new Russian friends for their patience, generosity and hospitality to us. I am so amazed to have done this that I don't think I say one word for the rest of the celebration. Dr. Veckler presents each of us with a necklace of ribbon, holding a piece of pottery that was of no use to restore. Certainly a lovely reminder of our two-week stay.

SATURDAY, AUGUST 14

Today is my last day in Moscow.

I am up early and it is raining hard. My luggage is put into the cab by 6:15 am and two of us are off to Sheremetyevo Airport. This is a forty -minute ride, but since the windshield wipers don't work we are stopping every five or ten minutes so the driver can try to fix them. This adds to our anxiety but nothing like the next booboo, which is when the driver asks us which airport. We try to tell him where we are flying to, but neither party understands. We are let off at the airport and find out that we are in the wrong one. A kind soul comes to our rescue and tells us that this is the International Airport #2, and flights within the country, fly out of Sheremetyevo #1, is where we should be. Scared out of our wits (by this time neither of us has any wits left!), we will not make our plane to St. Petersburg. We get into another cab and head off. We do make the flight, from an old scarred terminal, with no one around but one ticket taker, broken chairs, and virtually no lights. But we board, and my seat is broken and the wallpaper is flapping around when the "air" comes on.

As they say "Onward and Upward" and off we go.

P.S. St. Petersburg is a good trip. I stay for four days, and see it all. I'm glad to have made the side trip and when we finally leave Leningrad (another name for St. Petersburg) and fly to the States, I am sad. We love Russia.

We have several reunions in the States, fortunately, at my house in Philadelphia. The team shows up and most are in attendance. Nicole brings her husband, and what a delightful couple they are. We talk and eat, and talk and eat, and there is vodka and beer, but not to the extent we had been served in Russia. Such good times we have together. Two of my favorite people still live close by and we are still in touch.

End of adventure.

The Kremlin skyline from across Neva River.

The infamous Lubyanka Prison

Arbat Street—crafts, artists and musicians.

Russian Circus

The biggest department store in Moscow (all of Russia?)

What a puzzle!

It's gotta fit!

It does fit!!

A wooden sidewalk from the 17th-18th century

An entry doorway from the 17th century

Zadorsk Church—beginning of Russian Orthodox religion

Holy Water and open air chapel—Zagorsk

Chapter 10

1994: Canary Islands
Sea Life

INTRODUCTION

The goal of this Earthwatch trip to the Canary Islands is to work with sea life on Gran Canaria, the largest of this group of islands off the coast of Africa. We will be collecting fish, both skeletal and whole, to study, and eventually send back to the Museum of the City of New York. This will help the Museum complete their extensive files and history and preserve the specimens from this part of the world.

The development of Tourism in these islands has been made accessible by the construction of new roads and harbors. But this also means that there has been a huge "crash" in the island's fish population. With the surveys of two Earthwatch teams, our organization hopes to establish a Marine Reserve somewhere on the island and bring back the sea life, which has been reduced, and offer a protective area. The proposal for the Reserve will be given to the authorities based on our survey results. Tide pools and reefs are also endangered and these subjects will be addressed.

To get to the Canary Islands, one flies to Madrid first, and takes a smaller plane over to the island. (The Canary Islands are named after a dog– the star Canus– not a bird). I set out from Philadelphia to go up to Newark, NJ and then on to Spain. However, due to a bad summer storm, the plane to Newark has to be cancelled, and there is no alternative to making the Spanish flight unless one went by car. So I have to hire a driver, who drives wonderfully, but he and I are both racing against time. We do arrive on time for the international flight, but by then, the storm has followed us up the coast and even the Spanish flight has been delayed. So I sit, and the driver goes back home, and it isn't until 1 a.m. that we are able to get off the ground. Great way to start an adventure, but the alternative is worst (to go home and start over?)

And it is a dark and stormy night.... so we accept our flight.

I stay for two days in Madrid, and late on the third day, take off for the airport on Gran Canaria near the capital city of Los Palmos. The entire Earthwatch team is on the same plane, which should make it easy for those meeting us. But there we stand, with not a soul looking for us. Running through the crowd, a young man arrives holding a broomstick up in the air that has a sign attached saying

---

"Earthwatch come here!" Which we do, and after customs, all of us jam into our van and are hurried through the countryside and into a village on the southern tip of the island called Arguingin. It is originally a small fishing village, but has grown into a well-known resort area, with lots of boats and several hotels and some good restaurants. It is not Miami Beach, but the view of the sea goes on forever. We are staying in a nice little hotel, with clean rooms on a quiet side street. We are near enough to smell the ocean salt air. My two roommates are nurses from California, and are delightful. We all go down to the dining room for dinner, and then socialize for a while, but the jet lag is setting in, and we retire early.

MONDAY, JULY 4

It's always a bit unnerving to be in a country other than the U.S. on July 4th, and no one seems to care about this tradition that is so special in the U.S. I always say to myself– "How dare they not shoot off a firecracker for me?" They never answer. We take the bus over to a place called Porto Rico, where all of our work will normally be.

It has a parking space right on the water and our boat, for the scuba diver, is tied up next to it. There are no beaches here – just large boulders built out from the properties abutting into the water. Among these boulders, we will later study tidepools– one of our duties– while the scuba divers are out in their boat, looking under the water for fish and whatever else is swimming around. After lunch at a nice little seafood shop, we go back to the hotel, and are given stuff to read before a lecture to attend later on. It's very relaxed here, and also it is quite hot. I don't know what I had expected since we are right off the northwest coast of Africa (no polar bears here!).

That night, we have dinner up on the roof, where it is cool, and friends come to visit one of our assistants and it turns into a festive evening.

TUESDAY, JULY 5

Working in the tidepools has never really been my favorite sport. There are many tidepools here on the southern coast of the island, which is basically lined with rocks both great and small. In between the rocks are puddles of the ocean, which come and go according to the tidal flows. The deeper the tidepools, the longer it lasts.

Therefore, "things" begin to live in these pools and it is these that we are asked to document. Therefore, several of us go slipping and sliding over the rock jetties, stopping at many pools to do our day's work. We check the elevation of the pool below the mean high tide line. Then we measure the surface area, assess the volume of the pool, take the water temperature, (stick out your tongue, please), check the air temperature, the maximum depth, the salinity, (tasty?), how much algae, number of fish and their respective size. After all this is noted down, we are all stiff from crouching, and go hobbling on our way to the next tidepool. Thank heavens for the new Teva sandals, which seem to be anti-slip and anti-slide. After a long day of this exercise, we stagger back to where the van is parked, climb off the rocks, and drive back to the hotel to shower, eat, and resume our normal life.

WEDNESDSAY, JULY 6

Today I am assigned to assist in the de-skelating of a fish. Lucky me! This is the kind of job that I have always avoided, and have politely handed over to another person. Not today. Very carefully, with knife and gloves, I stand alongside the expert and look ready to help. I am fortunately used only twice, but now that I know (?) how to do it, I will be called upon later to do the whole thing. Anyway, when the operation is completed, all the bones are put in a bag so that later they can be put in a container which is filled with creatures that clean the bones of any flesh that remains. This whole process I find disagreeable, but anything for the price of research. This is a rather large fish, a 400-pound marlin, and one thing I will share is that the eye socket itself is the size of an orange. Enough said. Cocktail party conversation stopper, for sure.

We eat lunch with the others, and then drive over to our usual harbor, and go out on the rocks and look for tidepool denizens. Much nicer way to spend the afternoon.

THURSDAY, JULY 7

Today, it is tidepool duty again. The harbor here at Porto Rico is lined with huge rocks and there is no beach at all. This harbor is all boats and fishermen.

So off we go. A group of us climb up and down the boulders here until we find a level space where the tide/waves come rushing in and fill up the crevices. When the water comes crashing in, we all carefully step onto a higher rock until the sea goes back where it belongs.

There are lots of shouts when we get wet, but basically it is fun. One cannot begin to understand how these creatures/plants survive in these pools, but they have been studied for years, and they may change their sea-mates (pool-mates) once in a while but they seem healthy and happy. You may wonder how to tell when a fish is happy. I haven't the faintest idea, but they are swimming around and their world seems to be placid and uneventful.

Incidentally, we get samples of the algae by using a spatula and dumping the algae into plastic bags. We also, on some days, try to photograph the tide pool. Good luck and don't drop your camera.

FRIDAY, JULY 8

Today is our first free day, and we get into our bus and have a tour of the island. There are mountains to the north with the usual pine trees but also palm trees. These mountains are brown, which is a switch, and are home to the Cochineal beetle, which, when squashed, turns red instead of its usual white. This red color is used in the production of Campari, and is why Campari is the color it is. Also, a plant called Euphobias grows here, and is a relative of our Poinsettia. Go next to the town of Mogan, where we do a bit of rock climbing. Here the mountains take on a reddish hue due to the presence of iron, and there is also a green tinge, which means the presence of copper. All these mountains are volcanic but nothing happens while we are there. Hooray! We stop at Tasartico for a huge fruit drink and are shown trees that look like hat racks. The wild sage that grows here is good for healing, but one doesn't use it for cooking. And tomatoes are grown under nets to modify the sunlight and conserve watering. Then we stop at Miradon, a high point looking out over the sea, and watch the petrels playing in the thermals – rising and then plunging down; fun for them, not for humans. We stop at a cathedral town, Teror, to see the lovely church that sits on the village square. Every house has a balcony of flowers. On to Los Palmos to see the house of Columbus and then to the local museum. We walk around the old

---

section of the city and it is colorful and clean, and filled with old Spanish flavor.

When we finally get back to our hotel, we are all weary, but pleased, with our long day.

SATURDAY, JULY 9

Today, since there will be more boats out in the harbor and beyond, I am chosen to sit in the Zodiac while the divers are at work below me in the water, spending this morning videoing the reef and the fish therein. Our boat of course is flying the International Diving Flag, which means that there are scuba divers below, and to be careful not to cross or break their air tubes. One would think that this would be a no-brainer, but one would be surprised to learn of the common injuries suffered by careless captains of big or little boats who pay no attention to our flag. It is almost regulation to have someone sitting onboard of the diving boat to issue a warning, if necessary, to an idiot who seems to be coming straight at us. So I sit, with my little sun umbrella, my   bottle of water, and my sunscreen ointment, and read my book, all the while with one eye always on the surrounding waters.

Two dives a day are the requisite number for our project. I sit for the rest of the day, doing nothing but what I listed above. By the afternoon, I am sleepy when the dives are over. The boat goes back to shore, and I can walk around and wake myself up. It was fun, but I do not want to do it day after day.

SUNDAY, JULY 10

This is going to be fun. We spend the morning mending nets of various size and usage.   Then we make our lunch at the hotel and take off for the town of Mogan. The tiny village   has a good pier, and a good harbor, so we rent a boat with some other fisher people, and go out quite a distance, and cast off the sides to see what we can catch. The answer is not much, but I am lucky to reel in one fish, and they tell me that it is a very special kind. Of course – what else would I do? At least now they won't make me walk the plank!

We don't get back until after 4 p.m., but because of the fish, we are welcomed anyway. Our hotel cooks the fish (we all save the bones) and the owner sets a special table for our special feast.

MONDAY, JULY 11

We are up early this morning, and have to take the bus to Porto Rico– no car. Walk the rocks to some new tidepools, and work there for several hours. I'm getting bored with all this tiny, tiny life, but, apparently, it is necessary to the Museum's fish collection, to have lots of specimens from which to choose. Then we walk back over all the boulders to the town, and take the bus back to the hotel. We make lunch today, and then have to finish the net repairing–now or never. Several of us decide to clean the main living room where we all hang out since it is a mess, and we feel guilty about leaving it this way.

Our good deed is rewarded with a nice dinner cooked on a grill, upstairs on the roof where there is another sort of dining area. I am on dinner detail tonight, which means I have to transport all the dishes to the kitchen. But the dinner is worth it, and I caught the fish.

TUESDAY, JULY 12

Well, today I really did it! Everything goes well at breakfast, and then we all pile into the car and go to Porto Rico to do the last of the tide pool collecting. Fortunately, Laurie, one of my roommates is with us. We go over all the boulders on feet, hands and rear ends until we reach the desired pool. Just before we settle down for some serious work, I step back, for some reason, trip, and go down on the rocks with a huge crash. The wind is knocked out of me, and so I lie there for a minute, and Laurie comes (she's a nurse) and probes me here and there to see if I have broken any bones, etc. and seems to think I have not. But I am really in pain. So I know the group must move on further up the shore, so I renege on further work, and decide I will get back to the town and work out my future when I get there. Never have I had such a slow trip – dragging one side, which is where the pain is, and yanking myself up and down the rocks until I finally drag myself up to the parking lot. There is a restaurant here, and I go in. They give me coffee/water, whatever, and they call a cab for me. The cab arrives, and gets me back to the hotel (at this moment the hotel looks like paradise to me). I go up to the room, take off all the slimy wet clothes, get into a hot shower, and then fall on the bed to rest, until the group gets back. When they do, the consensus is that I have badly bruised my left leg and hip and should rest for several days. My roommates give me pain pills and I go off to sleep.

WEDNESDAY, JULY 13

I wake up and find I am still alive. Walking is a problem, but if I lock my knee so my leg is straight, I can move. Jim, our leader, from the New York Museum, takes me to his office and shows me some accounting work that needs to be done. This will save my life for I will feel I am doing something worthwhile.

THURSDAY/ FRIDAY, JULY 14, 15

And so this is how I keep busy for three days. I am even included on the ride over to Porto Rico each time, and once they suggest I come out on the Zodiac and watch for rogue boats while the divers go down and do some last minute work. I beg off, fearing I will be out there with the flag and the boat, and I am sure, a tsunami will come in and wash me to some foreign land.

On Friday night we have our farewell dinner together on the wharf at our little hometown here, Arguineguin. We have tapas, platters of very fresh fish, and some Spanish wine, and the frivolities go on and on. We leave, but not until we have stopped at an amusement park to take a ride or two, and then back to the hotel, and right to bed. Whew!

SATURDAY, JULY 16

We are set to leave. Three of us are going to Madrid to stay overnight in order to catch the next morning's flight back to the U.S. I am staggering around on my bad leg but get on the plane and off again without causing a scene. I head for my hotel, and am glad to be back on solid land again.

SUNDAY, JULY 17

Make the International Terminal in Madrid on time and the stewardess gets me a seat in the back where my leg can lie on the adjoining seat. Everyone is very helpful and I am as comfortable as possible. I must promise someday to do the same for someone who is as helpless as I feel.

And so, the end of an interesting trip, to interesting places – both of which I never would have seen and done things not usually on my list. I had a good time, met some fine people. I see Jim Tassel that fall, when I am in New York City, and he shows me the "fish" department in the basement of the Museum of Natural History where his office is. I can now look a fish in the eye, without cringing.

Porto Rico where we work.

The seashore at Porto Rico tide pool territory.

Doing tide pool collecting.

Waiting for the diving boat.

Divers get ready.

Preparing weight belts for diving.

Group picture of Canary-ites (us).

Scene from rooftop.

Roof-top dining room at hotel.

Celebration in the streets outside our hotel.

Bus stop.

Mending a net.

CHAPTER 11

1995: ENGLAND (NEWCASTLE)
HADRIAN'S WALL

INTRODUCTION

Hadrian was not only a Roman Emperor, but he was an architect and a builder. In Israel, he built a palace on the rock known as Ceasaria, and cantilevered it out over the side of the rock; he built another palace in Ceaseria, also on a rock, but this palace was shaped like a ship. This latter venture enabled him to invent a process of making cement secure, underwater. And then there was Hadrian's Wall in the 1st to the 4th century A.D. built in the north of Britain, in fact, across the top of England from Newcastle-on-Tyne to Carlyle. This was to protect "the neighborhood" from intruders from the north. Today, the Wall still stands, in good shape and in bad shape, and one can follow the direction of it from beginning to end.

Our Earthwatch project was to help the restoration of the site, at the Newcastle end of the Wall where there was a fort and a Roman military and civilian settlement to house and take care of the soldiers and guards when they returned from duty on the Wall or elsewhere in the north of Britain. The site operated as a supply base for work on the Wall, as well as a granary and food store for the troops. There were ampullas of wine and olive oil, carried by Roman ships, dumped on the shores of the Tyne River as it empties into the North Sea.

Our work would be in the fourth quadrant of the fort where, already, some preserved relics of the pre-Roman Iron Age have been discovered, but more work is ahead, and for that reason, we have arrived.

THURSDAY, JULY 20

Since there is no international airport near Newcastle, the closest city to my destination, I decide to fly to Edinburgh in Scotland and spend a few days before appearing for work on Hadrian's Wall. I had never been to Scotland, so I settle into a mid-city hotel and start out walking. I think I saw everything "on the list" including Robert Burns' birthplace, Holyrood Palace, St. Giles Church, the Fortress, Greyfriar's Bobby, the little black dog that laid by his master's grave forever. I also took a bus trip to St. Andrews and places in between.

MONDAY, JULY 24

Still in Edinburgh, I take a taxi to Waverly R.R. Station to board the train to Newcastle. It is a lovely ride through the countryside, with fields of yellow and blue flowers, farms and cottages. I arrive in Newcastle and take another taxi out of the city toward the North Sea to the village of South Shields, which sits next to the Tyne River and the North Sea. The village has fallen on hard times due to few jobs since the mines have closed, but there are a number of B&B's which rent to tourists. I stay in one of these and the landlady is Mrs. Elliot. The Earthwatch team had already gathered in her living room, so we sit and drink tea and get oriented to each other and our new accommodations. Our two leaders, Dr. Paul Sidwell and Nick Hodgson, introduced themselves and invited us to drive with them to see the site. This we did, and there is a reception for us in the building that houses laboratories and a classroom, and an area, which will become a museum. We then went to the beginning of "the Wall" and drove around that countryside for a while, then back to Mrs. Elliot's for a dinner, a bit more talk, and then upstairs, to unpack and go to bed.

TUESDAY, JULY 25

Our first day of work, so up, eat breakfast, gather our backpacks and set out to walk over to the site, about four blocks. We will become familiar with this neighborhood in the next two weeks, the well-kept single houses with the incomparable English gardens from one block to the next. Everyone grows flowers— you might think it is a cardinal sin not to do so. And the flowers grow and grow and are all glorious. It makes us USA gardeners envious and cross with all these green- thumbed-people around us.

We stake out several grids at the site where we will be working and photograph them as they were when we started. Out come the trowels and the small brushes and we start. Our supervisor is named Roger, a native of the area and a very funny man, with a brogue you could cut with a knife. We work all morning and begin to get the feel of our surroundings and of our new friends. It is good.

At lunchtime (although Mrs. Elliot has packed sandwiches and cookies for us), we run across the street to the general store (also the P.O.) for water or sodas and candy and exercise. We quit at 5 p.m., walk back to our house, have a nice dinner, and then realize we are all exhausted. So we go to bed by 9:30 p.m. No nightlife tonight!

WEDNESDAY, JULY 26

We are asked to shift to another spot at the site, just for the day, to finish up a corner, which had been left untouched by the previous team. So, like the seven dwarfs, we pick up our trowels and backpacks and brushes and measuring equipment, and tramp over to the other place. We did not sing "hi ho, hi ho, it's off to work we go" although several of us began to hum it. Long day but Roger keeps us in good fettle by singing songs by Robert Burns, which he also sings in a bar in the city every night. We must go hear this.

After dinner we all decide to walk into South Shields and see what the town is like. It is not spectacular, but it is nice and the people are friendly. We stop at the only supermarket and buy stuff to nibble on and soap (which is not plentiful at Mrs. Elliot's house) and some fruit.

That is the extent of our night on the town, and we go back and crawl into bed early. And nibble a bit.

THURSDAY, JULY 27

This is one of THOSE days. First of all, I excuse myself from digging for 45 minutes because I need to walk into town to the bank, to get some money. I am suffering guilt from the first moment, but go anyway. We haven't dug up anything interesting except a few fragments of something that was fragmented! How's that for a discovery? Even Roger is looking dour. And just as we are all groaning and moaning and we think it is about to rain, one of the older ladies in the group falls and sprains her ankle. She cannot walk and she is crying, and we are at a loss what to do. So someone calls an ambulance and she is taken off to the hospital and I offer to go with her. She is mortified that we are missing the dig, and finally, she and I convince each other that it is now raining and we would have had to stop working anyway, etc. She is strapped and taken back to Mrs. Elliot's where she is put in a chair, with her foot up.

Dinner is brought to her and she feels better about everything. So ends this day that wasn't much to begin with!

FRIDAY, JULY 28

The ankle lady, Maxine, who is a librarian in her real life, says she wants to go to the site with us today. Nick stops by in his car, we get her into it, and off she goes and so do we. It is a pretty day, and she sits on a rock near our digging. The first thing that happens is we find a stash of coins. We attribute our success to our brave companion, Maxine, who has now started slithering from stone to stone (slithering is not a good word— too snakey). She is scooting from stone to stone following the excitement over the coins, which has renewed all our spirits, and the day begins to glow.

In the afternoon, the car, three of us have rented for our trip tomorrow, arrives at Mrs. Elliot's house, and everyone is invited for a ride after dinner. We drive over to the beach here at South Shields and get a look at the water and the nice white beach, and the restaurants and the park, and wish we could move the site closer to the water. Then we drive down the shore road to see where we are, since our lives have been curtailed to Mrs. Elliot's house, the site, and the little town. There is not much to see in this direction, but getting away is good for us, and when we come back, it will soon be Saturday, and then we'll be off on a real adventure, going North.

SATURDAY, JULY 29

Free day, so three of us take our rented car and head up the northern coast of England.

Our ultimate destination is The Holy Island where Landisfarne Priory stands. The passenger in front does not know how to read a map. The driver can't take his eyes off the winding road. So I sit in back reading the map and conducting the tour. I don't know how we ever get out of our town. But we do. The miles roll by lovely farms and those special black-nosed sheep grazing in green meadows. In the towns we pass, the flower gardens are a delight, and every pole and post has a hanging basket of nasturtiums, mixed with baby's breath and marigolds. Stunning. We see a multitude of churches and castles, lots of Inns that look inviting, and old twisting streets with funny little shops.

We finally arrive at Landisfarne and it is impressive. The Priory sits on a spit of land out in the sea, and the road ends at the foot of a hill which one then climbs. What a spectacular place to live and write the famous illustrated manuscripts. Many of these manuscripts can be seen today in the British Museum in London. What a special display we see here, where the originals were created. We each decide we would like to rent the castle for the summer.

We descend from the site, and have lunch in a nice town nearby. Every little town has its own special pub, and this, in Alnwich, is truly special.

Back to South Shields for dinner and recollection.

SUNDAY, JULY 30

Another free day, and all of us pile into the van to go off to see the sites. Our first stop is Corbridge, one of the accesses to the Wall. Nick gives us a good talk about when, why, where, who, and how, etc. about life on the Wall. It is interesting and we now have a real sense about being a Roman soldier on duty here. No thanks! One cannot just climb up on the wall, like you would climb up a hill; there are only a few "entrances" that allow you to step up onto the path that goes along the top of the stonewall. Then one can actually walk along or sit and wait until everyone comes back to you. It is a fine place to meditate about those Roman times, or just look out at the fine scenery. I do both.

Then we are taken to lunch at the Bowes Hotel for a grand meal. I have lamb chops and apple pie for dessert.

Then on to Vindolanda where there are some smaller ruins, as yet not excavated, but where Paul has a small dig planned. Not for us, however. We now go to Heddon-on-the-Wall where the longest visible stretch of broad wall is ten feet thick. The stones here were originally set in puddled clay, but this has been replaced by mortar for stability. There is a circular structure in the side of the wall, used as a fireplace, or a kiln. The masonry used in making the gate in the wall here is reportedly among the best along the entire wall. We all bring some little stones back with us as souvenirs.

On the way back to our house, we stop at a cairn, which is a small pile of stones in the middle of nowhere, with a crater in its center, and this crater happens to be filled with Malllard ducks. This is actually at #42— Cawfields outpost. We stand right in the middle of the black-nosed sheep herd, who are bah-a-a-a-ing, and we are sure they were talking about us strangers.

As we near Newcastle, we also stop at Wallsend (nicely named) to see the official end of the wall and all the rubble around it. No trespassing here, so no more stone-picker uppers. We also pass a pub, once called the "Once Brewed" and recently renamed "The Twice Brewed". I doubt this is in the history books in Newcastle-on-Tyne.

We get back at 9 p.m. and Mrs. Elliot has salad and kabobs for all of us.

That is a nice ending to a long day

MONDAY, JULY 31

Off to work and the usual routine. I should mention here that archeology is a slow and methodical way of finding one's way back to another age or civilization, or whatever you are searching for. It is not for the impatient, since the slightest wrong dig or brushing can dislodge or disfigure an important discovery. Fortunately, the top layer of soil here at the Roman Fort (the Arbeia of the Romans) had already been removed before the archeologists (ahem! that's us) arrived. This top layer is called the Occupational Layer. When this has been removed, one can begin to see another layer, and below that another one, and this goes down and down. On my Russian dig in Moscow, we got down to the 17th and 18th Century layers. This kind of excavation is made with mechanical tools that can determine the dating from the substances of the layers. Many scientific tests can be performed with measurements and other methods of recognition, whenever the "dig" demands.

In our excavations, the site is divided into about 10 or 15 grids (small squares). We generally work in one grid. This sounds simple, but when you consider that the entire area has to have a pictorial proof of its existence, before and after excavation, as well as a hand drawn map of the area including each stone and crevice that is showing at a certain time — all this preliminary work takes time and patience— and all before you make one poke with your trowel.

So there I am and my trowel strikes something in the dirt that is neither a stone nor a bone. It is a Roman coin! Someone should have had a trumpet. No way. But it did make my day. Within five minutes, all around me are Earthwatchers concentrating so hard as they dig and brush, you would think there is a pot of gold just lying below us.

But the day ends with no more excitement.

TUESDAY, AUGUST 1

Today we move around to the other end of our grid, working on what is thought to be part of the flooring of a house. Scientists and archeologists before us have already read maps and histories of the area and have picked up many clues as to where things "stand" in this fort. I mean that literally. They have discovered where the granary stands, and the Governor's house, and in our area supposedly is a house on a local street. So this floor is probably part of that house. Five o'clock rolls around, and we have found nothing else today. So we leave.

WEDNESDAY, AUGUST 2

So— no floor today— but we move to an entirely different spot, nearer to town, which is an old cemetery. Now the rumors fly that we might come across bones or skeletons or fabrics (shrouds?) or jewelry or whatever one can imagine finding in a graveyard. So we dig, and then carefully sift the dirt we had dug, and then move deeper and deeper, and, by golly, we find a bone or two, both from a human body, but that was it! We are all disappointed in the lack of macabre relics we are expecting. What story will we tell the family back home?

THURSDAY, AUGUST 3

Two of us decide not to go back to the gravesite this morning, but instead go over to our fort where Roger asks us to find a missing book called "The Blue Book of Small Finds." I have fun doing this, in one of the more messy offices. It gives me an insight into this world of archeology, which is also important. Files, papers, and notebooks on so many subjects were piled one on top of another. And, of course, at the bottom of one of the piles was THE book for which I am looking. Everyone who eventually came into the office to find out how I am doing, thinks I am some kind of genius. I modestly (?) accept their praise.

As some kind of reward, for the afternoon task we are asked to wash the pots in the Find Room. It is nice and warm in there, which is good because it has turned raw and rainy outdoors.

At night, we are all invited into town to listen to the local historian give a talk about the Roman settlement here, and the monuments around here depicting heroic Romans. Then he mentions a similar site in Romania, with a famous monument that attracts lots of tourists. It is of Tragan, the famous emperor. Later we discuss whether this site in Romania might make a good dig, and decide it would. (As an aside, there is now an Earthwatch project offered at the Romanian site, near Odessa. I have not gone, but would love to know what it is like).

Later, we talk more about Romania and whether it would make for a good dig.

FRIDAY, AUGUST 4

This is our last day of work at the site. All of us are relieved. We feel we have done our job. By lunch time, several of the team have already disappeared, but the rest of us stay until 4 p.m. cleaning up the place, returning tools to the main building, and generally leaving no traces of our endeavors. One of the things that shocked me, at my first dig several years ago, was that all the dirt we removed and sifted had to be returned to the holes we made, or else the entire world would be filled with holes. Sites have been mapped, photographed, drawn by hand, and usually turned into grids (for easy identification) and so the records will show everything that was accomplished.

A few of us walk into town to get money at the bank for our trips back home.

Then dinner at Mrs. Elliot's and upstairs to pack up.

SATURDAY, AUGUST 5

Three of us take an early Metro into Newcastle and then a train down to Hexham. There is a nice church there and reportedly some good ruins and also some good shops. We buy food and drinks for our going-away party tonight back in South Shields. We have lunch in a small quaint restaurant and then "do" the church. I am able to talk my way down into the crypt below the sanctuary but no one else wants to see the tombs. We notice that the big organ is made in Erie, PA. That is a surprise.

Back to our rooms to prepare for the party. We have a fine time and get into further talk about a dig in Romania. For the first time, our leaders get serious ideas of going there. We all began to make plans, if this idea ever came into being. (It did!)

SUNDAY, AUGUST 6

Three of us take a cab into Newcastle in time to catch the train to London. I stop off at Durham to spend a few hours touring the great cathedral there, put my luggage into a locker, and walk through the town, which is great. It is a fine morning with flowers and birds and bells in the cathedral ring the time. Once we are inside the huge cathedral, we are totally awed by the grandeur. We then return to the station to take the train to London.

MONDAY, AUGUST 7

I have a two-day layover here and stay at a hotel at Heathrow for easy access later. I eat a delicious dinner as a present to myself, after South Shields, and retire early. Am up and off to the British Museum to check out the Roman relics from our site and almost shout out loud when I find the large glass case containing and describing smalls that look so familiar, but they will call the Bobbies if I make a scene. After my triumphal discovery, I go back downstairs to see the collection of Illuminated Manuscripts in the rare books room. They are magnificent, under special lights, indeed a beautiful sight. I go back into the city to walk around Buckingham Palace, a favorite for me, and then sit in St. James Park, also on my list of favorites. Enough for that day, back to Heathrow, another good dinner, and up to my room to pack again.

TUESDAY, AUGUST 8

I board a morning plane to Philadelphia. What an experience I have had!!!!

Hadrian's Wall (photo from travel brochure).

South Shield houses, so nearby.

Just watching Roger work.

At work.

You can see how one charts a grid.

It's very detailed work.

There always has to be a dog or cat on site.

An authentic stile.

Sitting on the wall.

CHAPTER 12

1996: SOUTH AFRICA (CAPETOWN)
WHALES OF SOUTH AFRICA

INTRODUCTION

"The overall goal of the Mammal Research Whale Unit is to monitor the status of large whale population in southern African waters and to establish the current dynamics by which an increase might be generated." So reads our introduction to the Earthwatch program for which we volunteers have arrived in Capetown, this year. Southern "right" whales were severely depleted in the early nineteenth century by shore whalers and other fisherman, as many as 12,000, it is reported.

In the late 60's the Department of South African Industries began a survey, by air, to determine how many whales may have migrated from Argentina, across the South Atlantic Sea, and over to South Africa and the Indian Ocean. This study was to show how genetically similar or different the whales in South Africa would be from the genetic studies done in South America.

The South African whales were actually named this because they were the whales producing the best oil for lamps. These whales are dominated by cow-calf pairs and this study will help determine whether the females came to this area each year to birth and raise their calves. Through DNA testing, this theory could help protect these animals, as well as provide overall restrictions to human predators and ship traffic

Therefore, the core of our research will be a genetic study, done by securing the DNA of individual whales. The specimens will be forwarded to a lab in Capetown for a continuation of this project.

SATURDAY, JULY 6

We detrain at the station in Capetown and it looks like a long walk to the station. I'm in a hurry to meet my new friends, so the baggage-cart driver says I can sit on top of the luggage and he will give me a free ride. I love the idea. I climb up on top, and sit there like an old-world peasant riding on top of the family hay wagon. This way, no one will know of my luxury surroundings for the past 36 hours, and I will never tell them.

And there they are: Peter Best (to become my good friend as we are the same old age), the captain to-be of our Zodiac boat, two students at the Museum, and only one other Earthwatcher— a teenager from Switzerland. We drag my luggage to the van and ride 3-1/2 hours directly to our first stop on our project. Winstad is a fishing village right on the point of land where an inlet flows into the Indian Ocean. It is gorgeous. We all make dinner, and Peter and I do the dishes. We sit around and get acquainted with our surroundings, and Peter explains our goals to us. We are all falling asleep. I get the "Queen Bedroom" which is a single and I am very pleased.

I'm sure we all lie awake for awhile, wondering how this little boat is going to work out, but decide there is no sense worrying right now, so close our eyes and sleep.

SUNDAY, JULY 7

We are up by 7 a.m. Ah, the sound of the sea! Over a nice breakfast, we are undecided whether to try to go out to sea today. There is a dense fog but by 8:30 am, the fog has lifted and we get ready to launch the Baleana— our Zodiac boat that although smallish, is compact and sturdy. There are many "swells" in the ocean however, and once again we think it may not be safe. We can see through our binoculars that there are several whales out there, resting in the water just lying there looking like logs of wood. The whales often lie in the water as shelter against the wind. Occasionally they spout, (we are tempted to yell "Thar she blows!") but we are quiet and wait for Peter's decision. His decision is no-go. We are standing in the water and can feel the soft sand beneath our feet, which is usual for the ocean where the river or inlet meets the sea. There are also some kelp beds (sea weed, for the uneducated!), which have an important role for whales. The whales fling kelp between their flukes to clean out debris including lice.

So, we go off in our van. We see two dead lambs in a pasture— victims of feral dogs. There are tall mountains backed up to the shore, but there are also palm trees and cacti. Aloe cactus has spiky flowers and the hillsides are strewn with them.

Such splendor. There are birdhouses called bird kitchens. Mist rises from the valleys. A sheepdog crouches in fear as we motor along the road. We are to take a ferry across a small river, but the stream is raging so strong, we daren't cross. So we back up and take a road to an ostrich farm. Our first sight of the farm is a meadow filled with baby ostriches. Too cute to be described. To the big ostriches, we give orange peels and apple cores, and as they stand and eat and look at us with their to-die-for long eyelashes, they are enchanting to look at. They have stand-up little hairs on their heads, which resemble newborn babies. Several mongooses (mongeese?) run around the ostriches and are also kind of cute— fox-like faces and little bushy tails.

We return to our house in Winstad (on St. Helena Bay) and find a stranded seal sitting on a rock in our front yard. Seals are sweet looking with sad brown eyes, but they smell awful and will bite you if you come close. We retreat into the house and soon the seal disappears. We opt not to follow him.

Our "water" day turns out to be more like a zoo day.

MONDAY, JULY 8

We're up early only to find that there is ankle-deep water in our kitchen. The water system has broken down. (I don't understand this African language so don't know what really happened). I do know that our morning was delayed, as we swept and mopped, and THEN had breakfast, and off we go.

I learn quickly how to take a boat over or through the medium high waves that are breaking on our beach.

You just go right through them and pretend they are not there. Equals getting quite wet, holding your breath, and I guess closing your eyes.

Steering the boat sideways through the waves, and heading almost parallel to the beach, but at the same time turning slightly left toward the ocean. Equals just as in #1 situation, although you don't have to close your eyes, because it's not QUITE as scary.

Do not even bother to try again. Rest on the beach until the tide turns or the wind turns, or whatever comes along to calm the waves down to a healthy height.

We finally get out of the harbor, into the quiet, greenish Indian Ocean. It is very beautiful. And there, ahead of us, lie two long log-look-alike things, which of course are "right whales". Meanwhile, as we motor toward them, Peter has put up a contraption in the boat that looks like a smaller version of a lifeguard stand. Up and onto it, he climbs, and sits down with binoculars and dart gun. He is ready when we get close enough. Then the excitement starts. Derek, our boat pilot and Peter, our leader, converse; the engine is turned off and we creep toward the whale. Peter shoots a dart at the hide of the animal, and when it hits the whale, it simply grabs a bit of the skin, and automatically, the dart is bounced off the whale and into the sea. This is where we, the crew, come into play. With a huge net we take turns reaching into the sea to retrieve the dart. Whoever gets it first, pulls it into the boat. The rest of us grab the dart out of the net, carefully dislodge the skin from the dart, and drop it into a bottle filled with a DMSO solution. Not possessing a chemical education, I take the bottle, without question, and put it into a freezer container that we always carry with us. Upon return to land, Peter will mail our "catch" to the lab in Capetown, and the technicians will go to work to extract the DNA from the skin of the whale.

TUESDAY, JULY 9

Up at 7 a.m. and on the Zodiac by 8:15 a.m. It is cold, cold, cold, and we are all wrapped up to our necks in our gear. In three hours, we are warmed up and begin to de-layer our clothes. We do not go out in the ocean as far as we did yesterday. We spot a number of males cavorting around nearer to the shore. There are five females in the area, and we suspect (but are not sure) that they are all vying for each other's attention. It is a good day, but no samples, as the whales are too active. So back to our house by 4 p.m. We are finally warm. A nice evening. After dinner, we play Trivial Pursuit. Derek and I win.

WEDNESDAY, JULY 10

Today, we motor quite far out in the ocean. It is chilly, but we are okay and end up getting sunburned. We have a sad hour or so, when a newborn calf (baby whale) loses his mother. Or maybe the mother loses her child. Is the calf just missing, or has it been abandoned? The latter sometimes happens when the mother realizes that the newborn is sick or deformed. Or the calf has just swum off while the Mother is looking the other way. (We all know our own children don't behave this way!). We spot one or the other in the area, but of course, we don't speak "whale" so have no way to communicate with either of them. We finally have to move on, never knowing how this would resolve itself. Later on, we see another mother and her calf, and they are in sync with each other, which pleases us. We take several samples— but not from them. Peter does point out a group of Jackass penguins to us Earthwatchers, since we will never see them anywhere else but here. I never did find out from whence their name came, but erase from my head the idea that they are stupid. How easy to use that term without studying the bird book first. And then an albatross flies into view; another bird I had never seen before. They fly like a jet plane— they soar and do not flap their wings, but just disappear into the mist beyond. Quite spooky.

THURSDAY, JULY 11

When we set out this morning, the water is very choppy and we bounce around for a while. Eventually, we eat our lunch earlier than usual, in case we have to go back sooner than usual. Our lunch consists of peanut butter and banana sandwiches, an orange, and a bottle of soda or water. Peter comes down from his "tower" later and gives each of us part of his chocolate bar. Chocolate never tasted so good! Then the wind dies down, and we are able to retrieve six or seven darts, which is great, since yesterday we had no luck.

A bit of entertainment for us in the afternoon is the appearance of a little seal that apparently is intrigued by this "thing" (boat) that is floating around in his territory. He dives up and down as he swims around us, and as we seem harmless, he then begins to do extra tricks. He stands upside-down in the water, and then comes right side up when he hears us clapping. Then he dunks himself again, around the boat, returns to where we hang over the side and go into his up-and-down position and then reappears for applause. We could have watched him all day. He loses interest in us eventually, and wanders off to find a new audience.

FRIDAY, JULY 12

Out on the water again. We are halfway from Capetown to Mosell Bay, which will be our last dart-gunning area. There are a number of whales here, and two of the juveniles come right up to the boat and look right into our faces. Apparently they are either pleased, or bored, because they only stay for a minute.

When one is out here on the ocean, the most important wish is that a whale, for good or for bad, may decide to "breach" when they go under our Zodiac. This would be a real mess if they did. The above juveniles were so curious about us that we fear they might go under and over to the other side to see if we look the same from over there. We did. So they leave.

I must mention here, that we ALAWYS have our life preservers on when we are in the boat. On chilly mornings, they provide extra warmth, and when we are in warmer areas, they do provide some relief from the hot sun. But no matter what the weather, life preservers are the constant rule #1.

A silly seal is asleep in the water. He is sleeping in an upside down position with his tail curved up and out of the water. Peter says that this is one way for them to keep warm.

SATURDAY, JULY 13

We stay in bed until 8 a.m. because this is a free day. Peter drives the two Earthwatchers (me and Ian) and a student of his, to the DeHoop Nature Prerserve. On the way, we have to cross a little river by going on a ferry, which is pulled by a native man, to get us across. I am horrified to watch this black man, hunched over and yanking us across, but think he has probably been doing it all his life and never thinks anything about it. We tip him generously and he is happy. We see many animals— mongooses, springbok, wild guinea fowl— lots of birds— spoonbills, mousebirds (looked like a real mouse but with wings), kites and plovers and stilts, and flowers— a whole roadside of aloes. On the way back to Witsand, we meet a family of baboons on the road, who want us to stop so they can get in our van and look for food. Peter warns us to ignore them, and suddenly out of the bush, arrive the baboons' relatives— sisters, aunts, uncles, etc. and even two babies. We do not stop as we are unarmed, and they begin to look sinister; Peter holds our slow speed, and as we get away from them, they begin to hoot and holler at us. Sore losers!

SUNDAY, JULY 14

Pack up our gear and head for Mosell Bay— a two-hour drive. Stop along the way to watch bungee jumping from a bridge. No takers in our group. Then we almost run over a cow that is wandering down the highway. Otherwise, the drive is uneventful.

Mosell Bay is a lovely resort, and we have a multi-bedroomed apartment right on the water. We eat in the apartment, but out on our front patio. The younger ones in the group walk into town, and Peter works on his papers, and I carve a tufted titmouse with my little knife (it even goes through the safety station at the airport). Like two old grandparents. To bed early after our long day.

MONDAY, JULY 15

In the morning, we wake to cold and wind, so can't take the boat out. Decide to do errands and chores. It's fun to shop in a town when you don't read, write, or speak the language— Africana is their language. It becomes a challenge of gestures, looking for the simpler way to ask for something or just drawing a picture. We go to a nearby mall to pick up gifts and food. Then Peter drives us to the top of a cliff that hangs over the inlet of the Mosell harbor. A spectacular view. All we can think is it'd be a great way to kill yourself, if you attempted to scale this cliff down to the water.

TUESDAY, JULY 16

Another "iffy" weather day, so we go through the mountains and over to Oudtshoorn ostrich farm. Rides on the backs of some of the ostriches are offered, and two of our group hop on. It is exactly like a rodeo where the cowboys try to stay on a bull— so did our guys try to stay on the ostrich. The bird kicks and swerves and the rest of us are aghast. Ostriches' hooves are deadly. We do see a mother ostrich standing under a tent with no sides, protecting an egg of hers that is the size of a tall beach ball. We do not go there! She looks menacing. Our next stop is a crocodile farm, which I am less than enthusiastic about. All I can say is that the young of any animal is sweet, and even the babies of these fierce parents are very attractive. However, I do not buy one (they are for sale).

Back to our apartment for dinner.

WEDNESDAY, JULY 17

At last we are "good to go". It's a long trip out of Mosell Bay, but we make it and are relieved. Then we see that there are no whales. We scour the waters, and even the horizon. They have vanished. Maybe there is a luncheon or something "way out" where we are not going. When we get back to land, Derek, our pilot, goes and buys a huge yellow-tailed fish for our dinner. He cooks it for dinner, and I make a big salad. Great way to end the day.

THURSDAY, JULY 18

Today we go in an opposite direction, and this route is just as long as yesterday. We pass two coves (no whales) and in the next cove, beneath the local lighthouse are all the whales! So this is where they were hiding. We work long and hard and collect 12 samples.

We apparently annoy one of the whales, for after the dart-gunning and retrieval, the whale decides to leave, and breaches as he turns, and when his flukes comes down, he slaps them with great fury at us, and we are all soaked. It is funny, but scary, and we have to smile at his reaction. It takes us a while to bail out the boat, and dry ourselves. But we survive and I guess he is pleased with his antics.

While we are chasing whales around the ocean and after we have retrieved the darts back from two of the friendly whales, one of the other whales breaks away from the group and starts towards us. We begin to panic as he draws too close. Derek stops the motor in our Zodiac. We two Earthwatchers move to the edge of the boat to get a good look at our arriving guest, and when he comes alongside of us, he raises up his head so we can see his eye and he can see us. We both freeze.

Our leader, Peter, calls to us to tell us not to be afraid because all he wants is to have his head scratched. His head is encrusted with stuff that looks like barnacles but isn't. Whatever the stuff is, must itch him alot. So Ian and I each take one hand and reach out to him and carefully start to scratch. The whale doesn't move. I am having some sort of epiphany, as I, 140 pounds of human flesh, continue to scratch 12 tons of whale skin and he still doesn't move. Ian and I keep at it until we are all "scratched out" and retire to the far side of the boat. The whale waits to see if we will return. When we don't, he swims away.

FRIDAY, JULY 19

To go or not to go? No one really wants to, but Peter insists. So we leave late, and grumble all the way. We now merely cross the bay. I have forgotten how spectacular the scenery is— great cliffs curving down to the sea like the back of a large animal. Gorges, in between, are filled with pale morning mist. The pale green water is so clear you can see the sand below. It's a truly idyllic scene. Seeing two Bedus whales and one Humpback (they are the whales who sing!) makes the picture complete. We turn to go back, and there are two of our old friendly Right whales. Wow! What a day.

On the trip home, the wind picks up and the water is very rough. We are bounced around like feathers in a pillow, and waves start coming over and into the boat. No one speaks, but I think there were a few prayers being sent aloft. Derek is a genius at getting us to our dock safely and we all enjoy warm showers and dry clothes, and then a good dinner of homemade soup and mussels.

We all fall asleep early.

SATURDAY, JULY 20

We all are up early. We are leaving Mosell Bay and heading back to Capetown. We start right away to clean the whole apartment so it will be left as nice as we found it.

Derek and Charles leave first and the rest of us follow in the van for the sad, rather beautiful trip back to Capetown. We go through the wonderful mountains and the farmlands with sheep grazing along with their lambs, and a bird we've never seen before— a blue crane— in Witsand, and perfectly blue-green sea. We will all miss South Africa very much.

Ian is put on his plane, and I will go later. Peter drives me around the city; I see the museum where he works, Signal Hill, Robben's Island (where Mandela stayed for 27 years), Tabletop Mountain, and then a slow drive through the city itself, and down to the harbor which is the current, classy spot to go.

By this time I can go to the airport, grab my luggage and board my plane to London. This is one time, I am truly sorry to leave where I have spent so many wonderful days.

Just looking.

The Zodiac (our boat).

"Thar' she blows!"

Please don't flip at us.

Chapter 12: Whales of South Africa

The "breach".

Sound asleep—like a log.

Here she comes to be scratched.

The long wait.

Chapter 12: Whales of South Africa

Well done.

CHAPTER 13

1997: SCOTLAND
OUTER HEBRIDES

INTRODUCTION

The Outer Hebrides is a chain of islands situated off the northwest coast of Scotland. The principal islands are Lewis, Harris, the Uists and Bara. There is a causeway linking the Uists but this causeway is just one lane wide, and therefore has numerous "layabouts" so that cars and trucks have somewhere to go when facing oncoming traffic. The Hebrides is both wetter and colder than the mainland, which is fine in the summer, but not so fine in the winter.

Our study is centered upon Milton, in Southern Uist. Milton is an 18th century town where Flora MacDonald lived, and which is the site of our excavation this summer. Flora is considered a heroine of Scottish history and therefore her cottage in Milton will hopefully be restored to its original state. There is already a monument to her, which helps commemorate her role in the aftermath of the 1845 rebellion when she arranged the transport of Bonny Prince Charles "over the sea to Skye".

Arriving in Glasgow was easy from Philadelphia. Only five hours and you are there. My hotel is so close to the airport, it is practically on the runway for the planes. After checking in and taking a short nap, I go to visit the Art Museum and then over to Glasgow University. Each of these buildings is good. Jet lag is beginning to manifest itself, so back to the hotel for dinner, and very early to bed.

The next morning, I ask directions to Ayr and the Robert Bums town and board a train that goes there directly. It is a nice little town, with a film to show you all about Mr. Burns and the surroundings. I have lunch in "his" tearoom, go through his house (he was not there!) and walk around the town green, then board the train and the bus and get back to Glasgow in time for dinner. Two other Earthwatchers join me and I will fly with them to the Outer Hebrides the next morning.

SATURDAY, JULY 12

We are all up early, have breakfast, and arrive on time for British Air flight over the Hebridian Sea to Benbecular airport near South Uist—our destination. We are met by the leaders of our team, get into their van and drive onto the main road. This is a joke, since there is only one road running the length of the Outer Hebrides, so of course it is the main road. We pull off into our first "Layabout" which is big enough to fit one car, and let the on-coming traffic pass. Otherwise you would be in a meadow. We reach a house on a lane to our left, which belongs to Angus and Isabelle McDougall and it is across the lane from their real house, where they live with children and two border collies. What a great idea; there are five of us in their "guest house" and the view from the back is mountains, and the front view to a long meadow which lead to the dunes and the Atlantic ocean. What a setting.

SUNDAY, JULY 13

We residents are up early, have our breakfast, and since it is pouring rain, we wonder what the protocol is for bad weather. We hang around the house, and the sun comes through about noon, so we quickly walk down the road to where the project site is, walk out over the moor-like grass and brush, and there they all sit, waiting for us. Leader Tim walks us around the area, pointing out where we will dig, etc. and tells us the background once again of this property. Next we walk down the lane toward the ocean, and sit on the top of the high dunes (these are really cliffs) in the midst of a field of daisies. There is an old broken down cart in the field, with the daisies, and we are sure we are looking at a Wyeth painting. Across the ocean, one would see Nova Scotia if one could see several thousand miles. On the way back to our house, we pick wild berries, make friends with several sheep dogs, and on our back porch are waiting two of Angus's roosters (from the barn in back of our house) and they seem hungry so we feed them Cheerios. Angus comes across from his house, and tells us that now they will be our friends for life. (?)

MONDAY, JULY 14

This is our first day of work and so we are up and out on the road to walk to the site. It's about 1/4 of a mile down the road but the traffic is nil and the meadow is shining green. As we turn left onto the path, there is a Lapwing sitting on a post, watching his territory, as we begin to invade it. A lapwing is common here, but not in the USA. We are impressed with his dark green body, his black head, and his tall crest which is also black and when he turns his head, the crest also turns and looks like the vane on a windmill. He yells at us, but to no avail.

We start right in digging. The top layer of dirt has been removed, so it is easier to get going. From where we dig, we can see the outline of this medieval town called Milton. The meadow here is surrounded by a series of small hills in the landscape, which indicates the possibility of an old wall, which would be in keeping with early maps and records. Flora MacDonald's house is on the north side of the rectangle, not quite up to a hill (wall?) in back of it. We are digging at one end of the kitchen, probably by the fireplace because we are finding veins of charcoal in the layers. There also seems to have been a drying oven outside the kitchen, for the wheat, etc that was gathered, dried and stored inside a barn or other room in the house. This is the fun of a dig, to a great extent, because you don't really know what you will find, and how it will add to the overall picture of the place that one is trying to restore.

At lunch, we all sit alone or together—according to our desire, and bask in the sun and the breeze that constantly blows in from the ocean. There are few or no trees on these Hebridian Isles because most of the year, the wind blows so strongly and the gales come along so often, that no tree can remain standing. We also lie in the grass and take a short nap before we are summoned back to our work.

I must mention that there is a "bully cow" behind one of the fences in our meadow and he does not look FRIENDLY. If we nap, one eye is always open to the possibility that he might come over and visit. Which none of us would encourage.

At night, we go up the road to a community hall, which has been lent to us, in which we will dine each night. After dinner, the young group goes off to a pub, and the rest of us go home. I am tired and forget to feed Tom and Jerry, my chicken friends.

TUESDAY, JULY 15

It is raining, hard, so we dress for the worst, which we find when we meet the others at the site. We define a few more stones, which means we kick a few here and there, between the raindrops and finally, we disband and go back to our houses for an early lunch. I don't go back in the afternoon because I am still wet, and instead, work through our leader's "Book of Flowers" and then his "Birds of Scotland" directory. Now I know what flew over us earlier today, it was a Marsh Harrier. Also catch up on my journal.

About 5 p.m., our landlord, Angus McDougall, knocks at our door and offers to drive us to a nearby town where there is a pub with good food. Great, and there is a tiny food market next door, so we stock up on necessities. Alistair, the only taxi driver in town takes us back to the house. Two Earthwatchers stop by to return eggs they had borrowed, and so we drink wine and talk computers. The wine is fine; the computers are beyond me. I'm off to bed. (It is still bright light outside at 11 p.m., so we all have to wear sleeping masks).

WEDNESDAY, JULY 16

Today is an all-day work regime, which we do eagerly because after dinner tonight, we are going in the van to a school near the airport (Benbecula, in case you forgot that name) to hear a lecture from Michael Harris, who is the top archeological expert in the United Kingdom. He is going to talk about the Vikings, and their first settlement outside of their own country. It is here on the Hebrides, not far from the area of Milton, that these seafarers went ashore and set up a place to live. Their homes were actually built into the sandy cliffs on the western side of the islands. Once they were secure in their choice of location, they had the ocean right at their front door. There was lots of seaweed and kelp that would wash ashore and was useful to the life that they were forging out for themselves. Gradually, these Vikings moved farther into the lands bordering on the sea and built farms and barns in the peat meadows around them.

The Vikings were also important for their introduction of Christianity to the islands. Today, the islands are mostly of the Catholic faith but the Protestant sect still believes that their religion was birthed on the isle of Ione, over near Skye.

THURSDAY, JULY 17

Another full day of work. We have definitely identified our part of the dig as the site of the outdoor drying oven for the wheat that was dried and then used as food. We also think we are on the side of a path which led to the back door of the cottage. There are beginning to be traces of the stone/mud wall, which was the back wall of the home.

When we have had our dinner, which is now officially in the community hall, the younger members of Earthwatchers go over to

---

the beach to play soccer. It is chilly here in the evening, and the rest of us are content to sit in our houses and read and talk. I remember to feed my chickens at the back door, their nightly handfuls of Cheerios.

FRIDAY, JULY 18

Two from the group decide that they will go to the island of Barra for the weekend. Barra is the southernmost island of the Outer Hebrides, and there is a ferry from South Uist. We all drive down to the ferry slip to wave goodbye. The rest of us go to a little hotel in the village for lunch, and then we all go to the bank and then go back to work for the afternoon. Dinner as usual, then chores and, of course, the feeding of the fowl (this is becoming a huge part of our life here) and an early bedtime. Tomorrow, we will take a long trip to another island.

SATURDAY, JULY 19

We all leave at 10 a.m. in the van for a trip to North Uist. We stop at the Hebrides gift shop just north of Benbecula and, of course, fill our backpacks with presents for our families back home. Then on to the "roomed cairn". A cairn is a small or large pile of stones, usually built on a hill, and out in the country, which is also a burial spot.

This cairn was built for burials. It is big and had been made into rooms, with shelves, on which the bodies were placed. Somewhat like the Catacombs in Rome. These cairns were beautifully built and the view is stunning. To get to the top of the hill is a hike, so we sit for a while after going inside the cairn, and then trek down again. This time, we are led to a little hidden hotel in the valley and take a path to see a circle of stones, much like Stonehenge, but much smaller. However, it has the same reputation for being the site of medieval religious gatherings. Even though small, it still has something spooky about it. We drive on to have lunch at Loch Moddy, which is a little pub with country decor. Good food and good fun.

On the way back to South Uist, we stop at the first castle (and last one), which we would see in the Hebrides. It is not very impressive so we don't stay and continue on to our houses and then on to dinner. We pick up the two weekenders who have gone over to Barra for two days, and find that one of them has lost her passport somewhere between the beginning and end of their trip. Too late to deal with it today, but thoughts of never being able to leave the island legally is a bit unsettling.

SUNDAY, JULY 20

Another day to ourselves but there is nothing planned, so I go over to the barn where my chickens live to see what it is like inside. Later, when I ask Angus, our landlord, if he puts his sheep in the barn in the winter, he laughs picturing the several flocks squashed together in the relatively small barn. I am concerned and ask if "they don't get cold out in the stormy weather?" He answers that the sheep know how to seek shelter, and the only thing he worries about is whether or not they will blow away. End of that conversation.

So then I wander about our backyard and walk down to the Loch behind us and just sit there looking out over the landscape, which has a certain primeval beauty. I find a sheep's skull that I carry for a while and then toss back in its proper place—the meadow. I meet Angus again and he is holding a young border collie in his arms. The dog seems frantic because he is lost. Angus goes into his house and calls the dog's owner, who rides a tractor over to retrieve the animal. The dog yelps with joy and squirms out of Angus's arms. It is lovely to know that these people know each other so well that they keep in touch better than many communities I have lived in.

JULY 21-24

This week is much of a repeat of what has gone before on the site. The Lapwings and the Oyster Catcher continue to scream at us every morning when we arrive. We dig deeper each day, and each day discover some new outline or boundary of the Flora MacDonald homestead, here in the tiny village of Milton. We do make two interesting visits during the week.

One excursion is to the site of a Viking project nearby on the beach. At a place called Bornish, where the Vikings settled and built their homes(?) sandwiched between deep layers of wind-blown sand, nine rectangular houses within these cliffs have been uncovered, with only the tops showing up out of the dunes. They were constructed in the local tradition of sunken-floored buildings dug into the sands.

Finds of platters, bone combs and pieces of pottery have been discovered. One always hears about the pottery shards that are found in excavations. This is one of the easiest methods to help date the site, since pottery has a distinct color and shape and was used at different times in civilization. They also uncovered a short-cross penny, which dates the Viking settlement between 1199-1216.

The other excursion we take is to see the Highland Games on a stretch of flat green meadow just down the road from us. Everybody comes from everywhere to see and/or to participate in this all-afternoon festival. They bring picnic meals, which are eaten sitting in the meadow and watching the contests. There are no vendors, no chairs, no trashcans (you take home the empties), no bands nor loud speakers. But there is cheering and razzing and all that goes with showing your support for your family, your neighbor, your town and your country. The big strong men lift weights, and some hit the gong with a mallet to watch the "Horizontal Thermometer" creep up and up to the highest notch. The lassies in their kilts and black slippers dance on the stage to the delight of boyfriends and parents, and the bagpipers keen and trill.

FRIDAY, JULY 25

The week is swiftly coming to a close. We have each gone down to the road to call in our confirmations for flights on Saturday. There is only one phone in this area, which is painted British bright red and stands all by itself out here in the elements. Just a stone's throw west, you will find a bright red British mailbox, which is one of the few on these islands, except in town at the post office. We are aghast at that fact; that these two services are so far apart. I think we are spoiled

If one stands at the side of this one-lane road in the early morning or in the late afternoon, you are sure to find yourself standing still for a long time, to let the flocks of sheep pass. They are going back to their own barns and meadows for the nighttime, herded by their owner and his two busy border collies. The shepherd has on his wellies and the sheep have their special black noses and ears. It is a splendid scene to watch.

We often are caught, after our work, sitting on the side of the road watching and waiting. It is lovely that no horns are honking, no one is yelling out a car window; this is simply a centuries old custom and

I wouldn't trust one of those dogs not to bite someone who broke this ritual.

We return to our meadow to clean up so that no one will know we have been there. The pictures have been taken, the stones have all been drawn, the finds delivered and washed and labeled and the Lapwing and the Oyster Catcher will no longer have anyone to bother them. It is a poignant moment when we are on the meadow for the last time, and two daughters of the MacDougall family pipe (on their bagpipes) as we draw near. It is misty that morning, and with the bagpipes keening for us, we are quite undone.

SATURDAY, JULY 26

We must leave early for the airport at Benbecula. All of us will fly to Glasgow and then spread our wings for other countries.

There are tearful goodbyes. While, like all the ladies, I am blowing my nose and wiping tears away, I see hanging on the wall of the little airport, a beautiful print of an Oyster Catcher, lying in a meadow of yellow wheat. I ask the clerk for the name of the painter and his address, which she knows by heart, of course, and when I arrive home, I write to this artist and eventually I am, even at this minute, looking at the best memory of that special place in Scotland.

Not exactly urban blight.

Between South Uist and the Sea.

The lonely beach.

Traffic jam.

Going home from the site to our house.

At work.

More work.

And more work.

Scrubbing the "Finds".

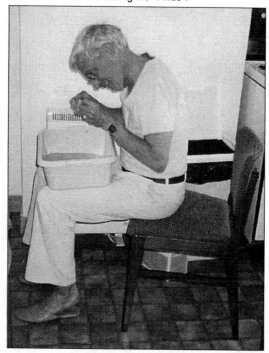

The buried Cairn.

A Highland Fling at the Games.

A man's game.

CHAPTER 14

1998: HUNGARY
COUNTRY MANOR

INTRODUCTION

We are going to a village seventy kilometers north of Budapest and I can't pronounce the name— Szarvasgede. Our project is called, "A Medieval Farm Revisited: Architecture, Archaeology, and Historic Preservation in Eastern Europe/Hungary." Where do they get these names? We are going to evaluate the structural condition and the history of an eighteenth century manor house that will ultimately serve as a research center and laboratory for an experimental farm. Students from around the world will be able to come to this experimental farm to study ancient crops and husbandry practices. The renovated manor house will provide the research facilities.

If you think getting to Hungary is a chore, wait until you try their language. Nevertheless, I fly to London from Philadelphia, then fly to Rome, then fly to Budapest, and then take a minibus into the city. As we drive toward Budapest, we pass a train, going the other way which must be a post office on wheels, for it has mail boxes lining each car of the train and there are men sorting the mail into the cubbyholes as they roll merrily along. Old world performance to us travellers.

Stay in Budapest to see the sights, and take time for the Roman Baths, which have been a "must" for years and years. Worth it! Dark, musty cathedrals, and monuments, and the beautiful river (separating Budapest from Budapesh) and lovely Herend china and, of course, good Hungarian food. Naturally, there is a group of violinists, playing native songs, as they move from table to table.

SUNDAY, JULY 5

I'm off to the train station to go to Hatvan, north of the city. I have a terrible time getting a one-way ticket, because no one speaks English. I think charades may help, but it doesn't; I'm sure the people in line behind me think I am a real nut. Suddenly, a young man steps out of the line behind me, who speaks English and Hungarian. I am ready to marry him right there. I go to the right track and sit waiting with a homeless man and his dachshund. The train doesn't arrive for 1-1/2 hours but I am glad to board and arrive at Hatvan, where there are two Earthwatchers already here. We wait for 2-1/2 hours to be picked up, due to a misunderstanding between management. We are eventually driven to our hotel in the little village of Szirak. (Why do so many places and people names begin with SZ?)

It's a charming place that was once an 18th century baroque estate. It has rooms for all of us, but we all share one bathroom— divided between the guys and the dolls. Showers are in a stall in some rooms, and basins also, but the bathroom dilemma turns into a comedy of sorts, but we adjust. On the front porch are tables and we will find ourselves sitting there for most meals, but there is an indoor room always set for dinner when it rains. There is a refrigerator in the dining room that is kept full of very good beer and wine. We are going to be well taken care of.

On our first night at Szirak, we go to bed early.

MONDAY, JULY 6

Up early, to have breakfast downstairs, and then drive off to the site of our work for the next two weeks. The site is the town of Szarvasgede, surrounded by gently rolling hills and many rivers and streams that support an intensive farming area in the Danubian region. The town has the usual modem utilities, but there are no trains— several buses, but basically no cultural venues. We tour the medieval farmhouse, which we will be "recreating" and hopefully, will become a research and historic center. The house is big with a large attic on the third floor. We photograph everything we find, and are told what our various jobs will be. It is a cool and lovely summer day, and we're ready to work.

But first we walk two blocks over to the center of the town to see where we will have lunch each day. The Municipal Building houses the doctor's office, the library, the administrative office, and in the basement, is the room in which we will eat our lunch today and every day thereafter. Two ladies from the church next door serve us and we are delighted with our Hungarian food. We buy stamps at the post office, check the general store, which also has groceries and gifts. We stand to watch the nest on top of the only telephone pole in sight because the nest is filled with fledgling storks and their parents, and will become our daily entertainment from now on.

Some of us will be digging, some of us will be scraping walls to see what's underneath, others will be measuring the outer buildings, and

---

some will be recording our activities in their notebooks. (No laptops here in 1998).

Back in Szirak, we get acquainted with the village, reappear in time for dinner on the porch, and then sit around and begin to feel at home.

I forgot to mention that the road into the site is actually a dirt path. At the entrance are two goats that one of our leaders calls our "Lawn Mowers".

TUESDAY, JULY 7

Today will be our first day of real work. I take the second bus, which gives me extra time to get organized. Three teachers from Wichita, Kansas and I are assigned to site #4 which is apparently the back stoop of the Manor House, and there is talk that there might have been a porch here. The four of us squeeze down into the grid that has been dug for us, so at least we don't have to remove grass and topsoil. We each start on the corner nearest to us since there's not room to move very far. We obviously get acquainted, and look forward to a good time together. We dig and brush around the stones and I sieve the dirt into a wheelbarrow. We extract anything that barely resembles something else and that/those pieces go into a separate pile. By noon we are dirty and stiff and have found nothing but a few bones. These will be identified later.

Lunch is, and will be, at the Municipal Building two blocks away, in the center of the village. We go down to their large basement rooms, wash our dirty hands, and sit at a long table. Two ladies from the church have cooked our meal and will continue to do so each day. They are so sweet, very modest, and very curious about all these foreign guests. We have soup, maybe a tidbit of meat, some salad, and ALWAYS POTATOES! We begin a game amongst ourselves trying to keep track of all the ways one can serve potatoes. They are served in at least ten ways, although never for dessert. We clap at the end of the meal, and the ladies blush, and put their aprons over their faces, in embarrassment. But I think they love us and we sure love them.

After lunch, we go to the store across the street to buy Mars bars, and then take up our to-be usual spot to watch the storks in their nest on the pole. No activity today so back to work.

It is VERY hot. We drink a case of bottled water in one afternoon.

When we get back to our hotel that night, we are hot, tired, and dirty, so wash up and go sit on our porch and drink that good beer. We watch the World Cup of Soccer for a while, but go to sleep quite early.

P.S. One funny thing we did this afternoon was to make bricks the old-fashioned way. (Maybe not so old-fashioned in this village). Anyhow, they are made out of straw, water and clay. While we are doing this crazy task, two men from the village stop by and help us. I'm sure we were doing stuff the wrong way, but they smiled, and cheered when one of our bricks came out fairly recognizable. The neighbors around here often come over to see what we're doing. I bet they go home, scratch their heads, and laugh.

WEDNESDAY, JULY 8

Today the four of us continue digging up the square area at the back of the house, which may prove to be part of a back porch. Actually, we don't think we are on the right track because we keep finding bones, both big and small, and what would bones be doing on the back porch? But who are we to ask? So we continue our shoveling, and our sifting; and we are acquiring a big pile of dirt off to the side. One of the ups or downs of archeology is the knowledge that, when we are through digging and the spot has been adequately photographed and also drawn, the pile of dirt is returned to the hole from whence it came. If another team wants to know what's beneath the surface, they just take out the file that has been made, and they can find out all they want to know without digging up even a tablespoon's worth of earth.

We have our usual lunch over at the town hall, and the potato soup lacks a little flavor. Well, we are hardly starving to death, and it's true you can't win 'em all. And the storks on the pole are all asleep because it is a cloudy day.

We are alerted to an important meeting tonight, after dinner, and we are all abuzz with what it's about. Seems one of our leaders, Lauren, had been called back to her home in Michigan, because there is a family crisis including a not-so-nice husband who has been caring for their four children and is about to leave the home and the children. We also hear that there is a rift between the Hungarian archeologists and the American team on how to do the work, and we all wonder if we'll all be discharged.

We toss and turn in our beds over the latest news bulletins.

THURSDAY, JULY 9

We are all in a tizzy when we arrive at the site this morning. Lauren is leaving at the end of the day; Mike, the co-leader is looking like a whipped puppy, and Irv, the third in command, is leaving after lunch for a conference in Budapest. Someone has to get Judy to a near-by clinic for her Coumadin checkup.

We decide that we will continue with what we've been doing (and secretly hope we don't dig up a treasure chest filled with gold— what would we do with the contents?). The silence amongst the Earthwatchers is charged with nervousness. We go on, finding bones and tidbits, as usual, and then straggle over to the village for our "potato surprise of the day". After lunch, we go to the cemetery next to the village church, and find this is a dead end (both literally and figuratively) since none of us can read anything on the headstones. The storks are sitting around, watching us, as we return to the site.

Actually we have a funny time together. There is a stream on the property, and we are sure we see leeches in there. We emit screams of horror and Lauren comes running over, and explains that what we see are not leeches, and. she picks one up. More screams, but at least we have broken the silence. When we are allowed to leave the site early, we have resumed our usual behavior and all is well.

Lauren leaves. We eat our dinner and go out on the porch. It is a moonlit night, and one of the group mentions that our village is very close to the mountains of Transylvania where Dracula had his comfy little castle. Everyone starts to tell rumors about the neighborhood here (they have caught on about me—that I am gullible and believe almost anything anyone tells). Within a few minutes, I loudly say, with false confidence, that if I see one (I stress the word ONE) bat fly over our hotel, I will be out of here so fast; you shall only see the dust I leave behind. They get a good laugh from this threat, and then we leave the porch and go to bed.

FRIDAY, JULY 10

We later call this Disaster Day. Mike has not shown up to bring the other Earthwatchers down from the hill next door, where they have been bunking in a B&B since we arrived. Now there are enough empty rooms down with us, and they are to move here today. It is raining and they had to walk. Turns out that Mike forgot them. We get the situation straightened out, and then he tells us that he has to go to the conference between the Hungarian archeologists versus the American archeologist to help them get along with each other. The van is stranded at the Hatvan railroad station where Lauren was taken to get her train. So here we all sit. We read and talk and try to nap on the benches.

Lunch is served, and the newcomers retrieve their belongings from the house up the hill and settle in with us. Mike returns and takes us with him in his van to Paszto to get Judy's report on her blood test. On the way back, we stop at a beautiful church and monastery. Upstairs, there is an art gallery of Hungarian landscapes. This country is quite attractive, once you get away from Sziak. We eat back at the hotel and Irv tells us, that to make up for our goofy day, he will take us away from here on Saturday and Sunday for a real treat. We each wonder if he means it, but nod thanks and go to bed early.

SATURDAY, JULY 11

We are off to Eger today, which is a city within driving distance of our hotel. There is a beautiful Basilica here and we climb steep steps to go in and look around. While we are wandering through the church, we hear the organ in the sanctuary begin to play, so we sit down in the pews and enjoy a recital for an hour, which apparently is presented several times a week. (And we thought it was just for us!) When we leave, we stop for lunch at a restaurant that has outside tables. It is a pretty day, so this is most enjoyable. Some of us have pizza, but we all have a pastry and an espresso for dessert.

There are lots of shops on this same street, but some of them are already closing (siesta?). We keep walking until we come to the Market, which is a large piazza with booths all round, and over this nice scene, is a real castle up "the hill. We walk up and poke around the grounds but the doors are locked so we can't get in. Back down to the market, and we stake out some benches, and then we ladies go crazy with our shopping— tablecloths, napkins, small doilies; everything that is embroidered by hand. One is more beautiful than the one before. The booth owners must have been very sad to see us leave, but we are running out of money and we have enough packages to fill a cart. This is what happens when you have been digging in a hole for days, and you finally are set free!

Arrive back at the hotel for dinner, we eat well, reminisce about our lovely excursion, fall into bed early.

SUNDAY/ MONDAY, JULY 12-13

These two days do not have any recollections or information in my journal. The only word on these two days is the name of the village, Szentendre, where our site is. I have no idea what went on in this time lapse, but I assume that whatever/wherever we are doing, it must have been either too boring to write about or I am being censored for my thoughts/writings.

No one, including the team or the Hungarian policemen will ever know. So onward to Tuesday, July 14.

TUESDAY, JULY 14

As soon as we arrive at the site, three of us are reassigned to go to the Town Hall and to the Mayor's office. What have we done? Nothing. We are to work on the files about "everything" which has ever been printed or reported about the house, our site, whether on radio or TV or memos or from local historians. We drag huge bags of old papers across the hall to their library and set ourselves up on tables and desks and start in. This is tedious work because we don't read the language, but gradually we evolve a system of sorts. With the help of the librarian, we are able to identify this conglomeration of papers by learning to read one or two or three words, which identify what the paper is about, and who wrote it. Of course the numbers are the same as ours. This becomes a nasty, slow job, and we begin to giggle at our efforts.

It is pleasant when the "potato" ladies call us to have lunch in the basement. After our fill of today's potato concoction, which is especially good, we return to the library and are joined by a fourth member of the team who turns out to be totally impossible in understanding our system and leaves in disgust. We do the best we can and when we leave our work to return to our hotel, we are still a bit bleary eyed, but actually, we enjoyed our new careers.

WEDNESDAY, JULY 15

Today we go back to the library, and this time our leader, Mike, joins us to see how we are doing. He also is confused by the task, but sits down and tries to help. The longer we work off some of the piles, the more impossible it becomes. The lady, who left us yesterday in a fit of pique, comes back and we wonder how long she will last today. Mike, however, to avoid another scene, decides to shut down the whole operation. Strangely enough we are sad to see this happen because by some mental breakthrough, we are getting familiar with the language here and it is beginning to be exciting. Our miracle is about to end.

After lunch, we spend time watching the storks. It seems that the babies are about to leave the nest. They are walking around the edges of their twiggy home and looking down on us as if they enjoy an audience. We promise them we will be back the next day.

THURSDAY, JULY 16

It is a gorgeous day, and when we get to the site, everything is bathed in sunlight. Two of us are now involved in measuring and drawing the barn, which after all these years looks more like a carport. One of us measures; the other one draws. Then we switch. All of a sudden, there is a shriek from the digging group at the side of the house. We drop our tools and run.

Two ladies have just come upon a bag of sorts, with COINS inside. Wow! Work stops, and we all watch as Mike goes down into the little pit, and very carefully uncovers the bag and the coins, and we all sit around and stare at them. The coins must first go to a building nearby to be cleaned, and then the expert coin man will identify them as to age and denomination. This will mean that if they are what we hope they are, the site will officially become a "place of interest" for the Hungarian historians, and will become another of their historic towns.

Our day is made. We go into town for our last lunch. Whatever will we do without our daily potatoes? We give the ladies hugs and small trinkets that we have bought for them. They are embarrassed, but pleased, and they try to convey how much they will miss us.

When we walk outside, the storks are putting on a display for us, which has us in uncontrolled laughter. The babies (?) are so large now they can barely fit in the nest. The parents have moved out and sit on the roof of the house across the street. The baby birds yell for their parents to come back and feed them; the parents yell (well scream) back at the two big babies to flap their wings and come over to join them on their roof. At one point, one of the babies gets up on the edge of the nest, flaps his wings, and then drops back into the nest. This sends the second baby up on the edge and he flaps around and drops back into the nest. We must have watched this comedy for a half hour and finally we had to leave. (We heard later, in letters from the staff, that it took two more days until the cowards finally flew).

This afternoon, another treasure is unearthed— a slightly dented old pot with a brim on it that makes it authentic. In our little pit, which it has been decided was not the back steps to a porch, we now know it was a garbage pit. Not exactly what we are going to describe to the folks back home but we have to laugh. No wonder there are so many bones in here. Maybe the next team will find something at one of the new grids that they dig.

At night, we have our farewell dinner, at which the kitchen staff sets the tables with tablecloths, cloth napkins, flowers in vases, and a special dinner (no potatoes) and even bottles of wine. We give the kitchen workers money and they bow and back out of the room and leave us to gossip and laugh, and have a final time together.

FRIDAY, JULY 17

None of us can believe that this is our last day until we are told there is still work to be done before we can leave!

We are still basking in the glory of the first coin discovery, and then today two more coins are found. Some people spend their time throwing the dirt back into the pits. If the dirt is not put back, in archeology terms, the world would be filled with potholes from all the archeology that has been done over the years. Two of us have to finish the architectural drawings we have been working on, so that takes our morning time.

We make a quick stop at the church, next to the town hall, since the "ladies who lunched" us would like us to see their church on the inside. The sanctuary has been opened just for us, and we are amazed how gorgeous it is. The lady who gives us a little tour tells us that she and her daughter have embroidered all the tablecloths, altar cloths, and other religious coverings. The needlework on these cloths must have taken hours and hours. They are perfectly done.

We check out the stork presentation for the last time, and unfortunately the babies are still flapping around, and the parents are still calling from the roof across the street. They will not listen to our pleas of more activity. But they WILL NOT FLY! Back to the hotel early so we can all pack. That means we all go to dinner in dirty clothes, but thankfully, there are no new guests in the dining room.

After dinner, it gets cool sitting on the porch, so we all retire early. Long day ahead.

SATURDAY, JULY 18

I am wakened at 3:30 a.m. by one of the team, and all goes well until I take my bag downstairs, and find the door is locked. I pull, push, and finally the handle comes off in my hand. (I should have gone back to bed) One of the other Earthwatchers arrive and she and I stand there and ask each other stupid questions, like what do we do now. Finally, I ask her for a flashlight and go down a corridor. The door is open, so I carefully go outside, down an iron staircase to the ground. I go to the front of the hotel and there is our waiting van. I try to explain to the driver. He doesn't understand. In a few minutes, one of the employees of the hotel opens the front door for us. Meanwhile our poor old black dog is totally confused and starts to bark incessantly. Everyone in the village will be awake now, so we squash into the van, with our luggage, and take off for the airport as fast as possible. A dramatic exit, I would say.

I sit around Ferighy airport and at 8 a.m., get on my plane back to Rome and spend the trip recollecting all that has occurred in the past two weeks. A good trip— no regrets.

Some words from the final report to Earthwatch

The focus of this project was the documentation of the Manor House in Szarvasgede, Hungary, from June 21- July 18,1997. The smell of mildew and insufficient lighting did not deter us. We analyzed paint color and stenciled walls and found silver coins. A hidden room was found after detailed architectural drawings. Additional foundations came to view as we dug around the house. A garbage pit was worked over while looking for a back porch.

In the attic, we found a treasure trove of historic documents, which had great insights into the development of life in the village, and in the manor house. In those days, the village was called Gede. Also, after the coins were cleaned and examined, it was decided that they dated from 1440 to 1444, during the reign of King Ladislaus. For the group who worked in the soil, particularly, there was a good group of seeds (they can last in soil for centuries!) and bone and charcoal. All research goals for this first season were fulfilled.

HOW ABOUT THAT!

The Manor House.

Back view of Manor House.

MY PIT! By backdoor.

At work.

Still at work.

Not for me!

Making bricks from the old recipe.

Now where?

Chapter 14: Country Manor

Lunch! Off we go to the village church.

Main Street. Third pole down is the stork next.

Is this Art? I think so.

Is this Art? I know it is.

CHAPTER 15

1999: CANADA (WINNEPEG)
COLORS OF THE NORTH

INTRODUCTION

The research we will be doing for the trip to Manitoba is titled "Colors From the North Country." The proposal deals with the collection, extraction and testing of plant materials available in Southeastern Manitoba, in Canada.

The proposal starts with the theory that most textile products currently produced, get their color from synthetic dyes, which are made by petrochemical industries. The uses of these non-renewable resources are chemicals that are highly toxic to the environment and to people. This is because to adhere color to the textile fiber requires heavy metal salts. In using natural dyes from plant material, it is possible to produce these colors from renewable sources— plants, trees, etc., without all this other stuff.

Dyeing fabrics has been done for centuries on wool, and often cotton and many of the colors that are used came from plants and trees. So these would be the renewable sources for which we will be looking. And one of the best places to find good plants for this purpose is along roads and fields and in meadows and forests. Purple Loofsterife, Swamp Milkweed, and Bog Birch are all well-known plants which most people think of as weeds. But their colors are brilliant!

We are to collect, then prepare the plants for dyeing, extract the dye, and then dye the fabrics to test for color. Nearly every color in the spectrum has been found heretofore, except for red. A good red is our elusive goal, but just the thought of picking a flower, preparing it, and cooking it, and discovering a delightful colored fabric as our end result, sends most of us scurrying outside to get started.

It is ironic that as I start on chapter 13 of my Earthwatch trips around the world, this one turns out to be the strangest-almost weird-adventure I ever had. The title of the trip "Colors From the North Country" is to acquaint us with a project to find natural dyes in the world around us, rather than use energy and money to invent dye colors for the petrochemical industry.

For some, the number 13 is related to poor luck, superstition, and generally bad news. I have always felt that 13 is my lucky number. Imagine how confused I become as the scenario in Manitoba unfolds in June of 1999.

MONDAY, JUNE 21

I have learned that far-away flights are to be made in the early morning (except for overseas flights) and so as usual, I am up before dawn, here in Philadelphia. I drive to our airport and park in a long-term facility nearby. The flight to Toronto is 1-1/2 hours late, so I don't get to the first stop until lunchtime. Thankfully, I bought a big sandwich and a large coffee. I fly to Winnepeg (our meeting place) and only find out later that we have the troupe from River Dance on board. Wow—I could have taken some lessons, if I had known sooner.

I meet the others (the Earthwatchers) eventually, and leave for an hour plus ride to our leader's house, which is sort of a farm, way out in the country. A slight gasp goes up from the six of us when we see where we are to stay, but our tired minds and bodies are more interested in having dinner, since it is after 8 p.m. We all decide to delay our reactions until a night's sleep, and that is what we do.

TUESDAY, JULY 22

When we wake up the next morning, we look at our surroundings and wonder how this is going to work. We are sleeping in two trailers that are hooked together to make a T; two beds in one and two beds in the other one. There is no bathroom for us except one across a little boardwalk to the main house. (It has been so rainy that the yard is a muddy mess; including the plank across the door of the big house). There are several large gardens, which we are to tend, and plant. A vast meadow is behind our sleeping quarters in which several horses roam, two dogs, two cats, five goats, two donkeys, and five geese. At least this all seems reasonable for a farm. There is a graduate student living in the main house, along with our leader Sheila and her daughter and a sometime visitor husband.

We have a nice breakfast— buffet style, and then we are off to visit a friend named Margaret, who sometimes helps Sheila (our leader) with her guests. We walk through the gardens, and then out through the meadows, where we collect lots of flowers and weeds that have color (mostly white and/or yellow) for our work back at our farm.

There, while we "cook" the plants in big pots on the stove in the garage, we work in the gardens, weeding, and preparing the soil for new seeds and plants.

The main meal of the day is to be at noon, which will supply us with energy for the evening and steady work will keep us from falling asleep. It works fine but it gets much hotter and so we retreat to our own quarters and rest and read until 4:30 p.m. Back to the stoves in the garage, and take the cooked plants and save the liquid, which has turned color from the blooms. AHA! We now have a pot full of dye. (Is this related to a "pocket full of rye?)

WEDNESDAY, JULY 23

Everyone is sleeping late and even after breakfast, we don't start working out in the gardens until 10:30 am. Phew— this is like half the day is gone and we are just beginning. It must look funny to outsiders (except there are no onlookers, this far out in the country) to see six women in a garage, working with huge pots, on a small stove, and clumps of flowers/weeds heaped on the tables, being stripped and chopped and tossed into the pot. We finally get a routine going and it takes three of us about thirty minutes to prepare a potful, and then we cook for an hour or so, and then strain the plants, but keep the colored water, etc. While we wait for the liquid to cool, we go out to the gardens and continue to weed and plant seeds under the guidance of Margaret, who is a trained horticulturalist and a great help in identification. Again, the sun is hot, so we retire for two hours until it is a bit cooler, and then go back to our garage duties, or garden plots. When we work in the gardens, we have to cover everything with hay to keep the birds from destroying our seeds. This hay covering is exhausting and we are all glad when that job is done. We have a bad, but short thunderstorm late in the day, and that will help keep the hay in place. Thank goodness.

THURSDAY, JULY 24

It is raining today, so all plant chores are cancelled and Sheila admits that she desperately needs groceries. She decides she will drive us to the next Province (Ontario), which is a bit of a "hike", but there is no alternative, and none of us have been there. The town is called Kenora, and is about an hours drive from our farm. We all pile in and off we go. This Canadian highway on which we ride is a long, straight road, with no curves or stoplights, but lots of farmlands on both sides, and lots of meadows, filled with yellow wild mustard plants (good for yellow dye, we think) and this yellow makes a beautiful sight for us to enjoy.

Otherwise, it is not a particularly exciting drive. When we get to the town, it is good to see stores, and restaurants and policemen on raised pedestals in the center of the squares, and flowers on lamp posts and no shaggy dogs, or seven or eight cats, geese, chickens and four horses. We meander about the quaint streets, while Sheila shops, and then altogether, we load the trunk with her purchases and set out for the straight-as-a-string road back to our farm. We notice a mother and a child leaving little piles of stones on an occasional slab of rock along side of the road. This apparently is an old Inuit custom, used by natives to give directions by pointing the stones in a special direction. (I am to see this later, in the forests of meadows of northern Manitoba, around Churchill). Now we begin to watch for these piles of stones, all along the road. They sometimes are quite elaborate, and done in different shapes. It makes us wonder just what kind of message is being depicted. We stop for lunch at a nice little Greek restaurant. We think about stopping to see a small art show, on the way, but the weather is turning really ugly now, and we head for the farm. It is now pouring. We run to our quarters to dry out. We have supper later and go to bed with the rain beating on the roof, and the branches of the trees outside our windows, bending and rapping against our trailer. End of a strange day.

FRIDAY, JULY 25- NO ENTRY

SATURDAY, JULY 26

Up early, and after breakfast, we are off to a farm auction in Reinbach. It's much the same as a farm auction at home in Pennsylvania. Sheila buys some stuff while the rest of us poke around and wonder what we are doing here, and is this really part of our work project. On the way back, we stop for groceries, and then Sheila takes us to see a Mennonite Village nearby. This is fun, if one has never seen the Mennonites and their homes and communities, but I am also familiar with this sight, since I live near the Amish people, in Lancaster, PA, and the Mennonites, in that area, are a similar sect to the Amish. We have lunch at the simple table and enjoy their special kind of food— which is always good and always plentiful. Today, it is borsht bread and homemade cheese, and home-baked cookies.

On the way back to the farm, we stop at another auction (nothing here but junk) and we are aware of the rivers and streams about to overflow after the recent severe storms and wonder if the streams on the farm are bubbling over, too. They are. So for the afternoon, we "cook" some more plants and dye a few more pieces of wool, and end when the sun disappears. We go to our trailers and read until dinnertime. Dinner is, unfortunately, really delayed due to the visit of a Mr. Churchman, at 8 p.m., with three children and a wife and they do not leave until 10 p.m. We, of course, cannot join in the conversation going on between Sheila and her guests, since the chatter is all about local life and general news of the neighborhood. We are totally out of touch with all this. We are also totally out of food and totally starving. As soon as the Churchman family leaves, we all leap toward the kitchen and start making grilled cheese sandwiches on the grill. Sheila comes into the room and goes into a huge rage at our behavior. She stamps out of the room, we eat our sandwiches, and head for our sleeping quarters, wondering what in the world is going on here????

SUNDAY, JUNE 27

We are all up by 8 a.m., and go over to the farmhouse. There is no one there. Sheila, her husband, Frank, and her daughter, Megan are missing. So we all make breakfast, and sit around and wait and watch and wonder. Meanwhile, I go outside, and notice that one of the horses has managed to get out of the coral, and is standing around (like us) wondering what he should do. None of us humans want to catch the horse, not knowing this horse's personality, and not caring to find out. Finally my friends(?) decide I am the chosen one, to talk to the horse and persuade him to return to his own territory. I approach— he steps away— I walk closer— he steps farther back— this little performance goes on for 10 minutes. We are getting nowhere. I am getting annoyed, so I bypass his head, pull alongside his head, grab his mane, and raise my voice. He looks startled and backs right through the gate, which I slam shut. Then I look over the fence, right in his face (now I am very brave!), tell him how naughty he has been, and walk away. The other horses look at him in disbelief. Go figure.

At noon, the three fugitives appear; Sheila is still in a huff, so Frank, Megan, and several of us scrape together a cooked lunch of pirogues, bread, salad, and ice cream. Then we clean up.

In the afternoon, still no Sheila, so we go to the garage and cook up some plants, and even dye our pieces of wool. We are making a "Thrum", which is a large ring of wood and to the circle we add each piece of wool we have dyed, arrange all of them according to color or a different shade of the color next to it, and gradually accumulate what looks like a huge ring of keys— only the keys are pieces of wool strung together into a color wheel. Quite a pleasing result, and one that we will all take home to show our friends.

Back to the journal. Go to the farmhouse for supper— still no Sheila. Frank sits with us and tells us not to feel guilty. Megan bakes us the best carrot cake we have ever tasted. We are all at a loss to know what to do. We go back to our cabins, talk for a long time, and decide that we will leave this place tomorrow.

As for me, I do not know what is the right or wrong thing to do. We could call Headquarters, but there is only one phone on the property. The phone is in Sheila's room and no one is going in there! So we close our eyes to the confusion about us and try to sleep.

MONDAY, JULY 28

We are awake by 7 a.m., go over to the farmhouse and have breakfast. No one is there, so we make our own meal. Sheila finally comes out of her room and announces that "it is time to go and you must go and get your boots on." One of the more aggressive Earthwatcher stands up and says, "Yes, it is time to go, but we are not going with you—we are going home." Dead silence. Sheila is shocked (I can't imagine she didn't suspect something like this). There follows fifteen minutes of yelling and screaming and when it is over, we are told be ready by 9:15 a.m. and we will be driven to the airport. We troop out and soon are in the bus, and on our way to Winnipeg.

We arrive and spend hours getting all our reservations changed. Then we sit around for six hours (I am one of the last to go), eating, reading, watching the people, and otherwise staring into space wondering why we are here, and what have we done. I finally board a plane to Chicago which goes through a violent thunderstorm. I feel that perhaps the Gods are angry with us. Eventually get back to Philadelphia, albeit, it's the middle of the night. But it's home!

We all fill out our reports for Earthwatch and our stories must have had the same scenario. Quickly, we hear back from Earthwatch that another person had been sent out to Winnipeg to see the place and the people. He came back with a glowing report. I wonder if Meg made him her carrot cheesecake, and if that made his report so good. We will never know.

The Farmhouse.

More farm.

Sowing seeds.

More farm.

Chapter 15: Colors of the North

Canadian highway—straight as an arrow.

CHAPTER 16

2000: CANADA (CHURCHILL)
CLIMATE CHANGE AT ARCTIC'S EDGE

INTRODUCTION

With the documented global warming that is occurring today, it is anticipated that areas with the largest annual range will be impacted first and foremost. Our area of study consists of open forest and forest tundra and shrub tundra. The northern forests are characterized as high concentration of peat deposits which in turn is a significant buffer for atmospheric carbon, which is directly related to global warming. We will be establishing six research sites for long-term monitoring in relation to treeline stability and climate change. Three plots will be in the forest including a mature site, a burned site and a planted site.

The top priority to the town of Churchill is the sustainable use of natural resources and the natural environment. It will turn into an intensive monitoring project. Volunteers will help to collect data on permafrost, soils, lichens and mosses, mammal, bird and insect censuses. Participants will spend about 50% of their time on forest study, and other 50% on tundra studies.

Ready, set, go. (I should have brought long underwear!)

TUESDAY, JUNE 27

The briefing notebook has suggested that we bring plenty of warm clothing to be layered, hiking boots, gloves, hats, etc. so we will be comfortable in the weather we will find in Churchill, Manitoba, Canada. In Philadelphia, on this Tuesday morning, the temperature is already almost 80 degrees and will climb into the 90's by the afternoon. I think to myself that if I walk through the airport terminal, in winter clothes, including boots, I am sure to be carted away in a straitjacket, and put behind bars. I pack a few warmer things, just to show my good faith. I fly to Toronto, then quickly over to Winnepeg, and from there, I am to be flown by CALM airways up to Churchill. However, that flight is cancelled at 3 p.m. when word comes that Churchill is having a blizzard, and no planes can land. Snow in June???? So the Earthwatch members of Team #11 go off to the airport hotel to spend the night. We all have dinner together that evening, which is nice, since no one knows each other, and we are all in this together.

WEDNESDAY, JUNE 28

Up early and back to the airport, and onto the plane headed north. We arrive in Churchill about 10 a.m. and are met by Peter Scott, our leader, and one of his assistants. Into town we drive, and wait while they go grocery shopping, and then out of town and over miles of tundra to the Churchill Northern Studies Centre. This building had originally been a tracking station for NASA and there is a tall rocket sitting on the front yard of the Centre. My expectations are always 180 degrees off when I arrive in a new place, and it happens again. I gape. There are bars on all the windows, and on the front door is the sign we have all been warned about... the footprint of a polar bear, with the words "STOP" and "POLAR BEAR ALERT". It is getting cold out here. Am I completely out of my mind? Probably, but I am stuck here and so "onward".

When we get inside the Centre, we are told that the Centre has kept the barracks kitchen part of the NASA facility and did some work on what is now the hub of the scientific work that goes on around here. We sleep six to a room— three bunk beds and I ask for a lower bed. Request granted. We have to share the bathroom with all the other women sleeping here, two toilets, two basins, and two showers. I think, oh no, but everybody seems to just be cool with it, and get out of the bathroom ASAP. We eat lunch that day in the cafeteria, with the open kitchen, and a young man who loves to cook, does all the honors. There is always juice and coffee available, and a bowl of fruit and peanut butter and jelly, in case you are in the last throes of starvation. Dinner is early, at 5:30 p.m. each day, but we learn that this is good because everyone gets sleepy early being out in the cold air during the day.

Peter, our leader, takes us into the classroom after lunch, and tells us what we will be doing, and where and why, and how. Then he takes us out to some of the sights where we set traps to see if we can catch something.

When we go back to the station, we meet an Audubon group of bird watchers, who seem to think we know little, and they know a lot. We soon learn that one of "ours" — a 16 years old boy—can out-bird any one of that other group, with no problem. We are delighted that he is on our team!

THURSDAY, JUNE 29

Peter takes us all back to the forest and maps out meters with flags, and puts down more traps. Once all that is done, we leave the forest and go to see some cement blocks which are being tested for their durability in this climate. Some have crumbled or cracked, but some have been there for twenty years, and are still standing. This kind of test and knowledge is important to people here, particularly when they are erecting buildings or building other kinds of docks, roads, installations, etc. We stop at one of the Twin Lakes to eat our boxed lunches and, for a while think, we might take a dip in the water. One hand in the water satisfies our wishes quickly— it is very cold. I mean very cold. Next we go to another site where, last year, there was a fire. We map out that area as well, with flags, etc. One slightly jarring note is that each time we stop to do work, one of our team is put on "Bear Alert", given a gun, and slowly walks around and around the area, in case of a sighting. We think at first that this was a little much, but as we get further into the life here, we realize that this is indeed a necessity. We are to hear stories of careless actions and of unpleasant endings.

Back to the Centre, and then out on the tundra at the other side of the building. Here we map out more areas for study and do special tests.

That night, we almost eat out the kitchen since we have been out all day and are close to starvation.

INSERT FOR JUNE 29

Today we have a lecture, and we are beginning to learn all new stuff.

Peat absorbs the carbon in the air.

There are no swamps here, but there are fens of tamarind and larch; bogs of black spruce and tree ash.

The forest is free of abrasion.

The tundra is damaged by wind.

Tremendous diversity here in Churchill.

Roots make the difference; cold roots can't absorb nutrients; temperature, more than anything controls growth here. If the peat gets too hot or dry to protect them (which I gather it is doing) trees can grow in the snowmelt of spring.

The tree line, in global warming, is going to come down to us in our Northern Hemisphere.

A fen has thinner peat, but its own water; a bog has more peat, but no water of its own. A bog is very acidic and can therefore turn into a salt marsh.

There are 80 ft. icebergs in Hudson Bay.

It is 2170 miles to the North Pole, the same as from Churchill to Orlando, Florida. I had asked if we could go to the North Pole, on our day off? (Shows how smart I am!)

It takes 100 days for ice to unfreeze, in a year

Now back to simple talk. The corridors in the Centre, to which we go, for lectures, computer work, kitchen and food, have polar bear paw-prints all along the floor. And there are pictures of bears all over. In the reception room is a stuffed polar bear, who would not fit on your bed, or in your living room. Its feet are bigger than dinner plates.

We drive into town for supplies, and on the way, see caribou by the road. On our left, on the Bay is a huge foreign freighter, which was grounded here in 1961. It still sits where it landed. A gyrfalcon has been nesting in its smoke stack ever since, but the ship has begun to sway a bit, and apparently this is unnerving the bird. The boat is beginning to sink, and will fall over on its side soon. The bird knows this, and we all hope he gets out of there in time, with his family and friends.

On the way back from town we see lots of other birds— harlequin duck, eider, arctic tern, shoveler, whimbrel, greater scaup, robin and even a raven. Our genius 16 year old is "our man of the bird watch" that day.

FRIDAY, JUNE 30

We start the day (after a very good breakfast) by going back into our first forest to check on the traps, and I, for one, am glad there are no animals in the traps. Then we go off to the "burned site", mapping out the places where we will dig next week.

We do some probe tests on the tundra site, measuring the depth of the peat before one hits the perma frost. It is awfully cold out there, and when it is time for lunch, we quickly go back to the Centre, and have hot soup, and more hot soup, and finally, we warm up.

For the afternoon, we set up the computers, working on how we are going to document all our findings and measurements, etc. for future teams. At this point, I can only help by reading information to two of the guys who know what they are doing as I am quite "computer" stupid. But I am learning. When we finish with the computers, we go outside, and count, down on our hands and knees, "willows" and some other plants. It is still freezing, so Peter gets us all in the van and takes us into Churchill, and over to Morrey Point, on the river, where there are lots of Beluga whales. In between all the whales, and icebergs, swim some eiders (whose down goes into pillows). We see our first arctic hare, which is just an oversized American rabbit, but he looks at us as if to say, well, that's YOUR story!

Along the road back, we stop at a park with a monument in its center, of a Chipequa Indian lady, who sold herself as a slave to an enemy tribe, in order to make peace between them and her own tribe.

SATURDAY, JULY 1

We wake up this morning to the smell of bacon, throughout the whole building— very good! Outside, we are going to work in the peat bog again. Problem is that it is not only cold, but it is sleeting. But we are brave, and continue using our testing probes to chart the depth of the peat before one hits the permafrost. One of us probes and one of us stands by to help read the depth, and then enter it into our little record book. None of us can decide which is worse— using the probe (at least one was bent over, a bit out of the wind), or to stand and record in the book and one need not be bent over the bog. Neither is preferable. We work all morning, and at lunchtime, race back to the warmth of the Centre and devour anything that is heated.

After lunch we go back to the bogs and start again. We look up at Peter expecting him to turn into Simon Legree. He doesn't. No whip! After a while, even Peter gets cold, and so offers to drive any of us who wants, into town to see their celebration of Canada Day. The

Polar Bear swimming event has been cancelled due to the weather, and the wind is blowing so hard that the softball game is also cancelled.

Like most of the team, I opt to stay at the Centre and drink hot coffee. The van returns in less than 1-1/2 hours. The temperature out side is 31F and the wind chill is 21 F. One female in our group planned to do the swimming event, but since it is called off, we never have the chance to find out if she really would have done it.

Enough of this! Just remember that this day is the first day of July!

SUNDAY, JULY 2

Weather-wise, just like July 1, so all is cancelled and we spend the day reading, organizing our rooms, catching up on computer work, and keeping warm.

MONDAY, JULY 3

Work at the computers most of the morning. Before lunch we go out to work on the plants.

There are a surprising number of plants which grow in this climate. The problem is that they do not grow more than about five or six inches high. Any higher, and they would be blown away. It amazes all of us to see the trees here; they are generally pine trees, and have no branches on the side that are toward the wind. The other sides of a pine tree have regular branches, as we know them. One gets used to seeing their lopsided profile. And the plants are the same. We make grids of the area in which the most plants were growing— short rhododendrons, daisies, mosses and lichens (ground covers), many species of vascular plants (which can weather this extreme weather), little purple flowers which none of us are familiar with, and a host of other tiny shrubs which also enjoy this climate, but stay lowdown.

While we are out doing this plant project, I ask Peter if I can draw these grids the way I'd been taught in other archeology trips. He says yes, and I am hired. I now feel that I am really contributing something different to our project. So I stand over all the little plots and draw the outlines of each. We treasure every little bud and flower and although my fingers go numb, once in a while, I am having a great time. That evening, I transpose all my notes onto a

---

grid using their projector light to see through the paper. Very clever, I say to myself.

We go on another bird trip because this is Monday Night Bird Count. We see a few new birds, but not a really productive trip. On the way back to the Centre, Peter drives up over the tundra to show us one of the famous Tundra Buggies. It looks like a regular big, fat, bus but it has VERY LARGE TIRES to give it plenty of support. And the windows are high enough off the ground so that no polar bear who might want to eat you, could reach your window, even standing on his back feet. Some consolation in case of an unplanned encounter,

TUESDAY, JULY 4

This is our day off. We leave early to drive to Goose Creek to see where our water originates. There's plenty of seawater around here, but we don't drink it. Later on we find out a very important use for it. We see a new marina, the granary, which is where grains are stored (what else?). It is quite an industry here. There are some new shore birds and then we are all let off at North Sea Tours, in the center of town, where we are booked on a 1 p.m. whale trip.

We have some time to browse around the town, to eat some lunch, buy some provisions and souvenirs. There are more saloons than grocery stores, but also two wonderful little museums. We make the most of our free time.

At the marina, we put on our life jackets, which are nice and warm, and then huddle down into our Zodiac (a large, rubber boat about 8 or 10 feet long, with high sides, and plenty of foot room, and notably safe and strong). There are lots of icebergs in the Churchill River and we dodge around them and stare in wonder at these beautiful gigantic pieces of ice. Seen from different angles, they have inner colors of blue and pink, and look quite otherworldly. But we are really here to see the whales. They soon come, looping up and down in the wake of our boat, and entertaining us as if they are on stage. They certainly are. There is also a single seal that follows us, and then looks back at us constantly, as he swims away. There are arctic terns, jaegers, and some Franklin gulls.

All of a sudden, our skipper looks up at sky, radios back to land, and we go into swift retreat mode. Heavy, black clouds have appeared and it looks very stormy. One does not want to be out on the bergybit (old sea term?) river in a Zodiac in a storm. We make it in time and don't lose our trip money. Again, we gather at a restaurant, and drink coffee and tidbits, do some more shopping, and are picked up by the van in late afternoon.

We wonder why we are heading towards the airport. Aha! Now we will see where the bad polar bears go when they misbehave here on land. There are three unused buildings— old hangars— side by side— with 9 cells in each one. When the bears become annoying or dangerous (they have pushed open saloon doors, peeked into private home windows, lumbered down a street looking for something or someone to attack, or are just to terrify, and/or maybe they are just bored) they are sedated by the police, put onto a truck and relocated to the jail and are put in a cage for the summer... until Hudson Bay freezes over again, and then by reverse methods, are let free on the ice. They are in hibernation for this period and do not eat any food, but must be supplied with melted seawater— a constant to their survival. All I can imagine is how one does this. Certainly not in a beach pail, which is the only way I know. Meanwhile, the females have dug their dens, produced their children, taken good care of them and are ready to reappear when the new ice appears.

We arrive back at the Centre, have dinner, and then go out and build a snowman of new-fallen snow and have our picture taken to prove to unbelievers, back home, that we REALLY did this. I do the face. Finally, we come inside and do some crazy antics outside the Quiet Room, where a message is waiting for all of us from Earthwatch, back in Massachusetts, who insists that we must be very careful while we are up here and not to do anything silly, and to obey all the rules!

End of a great day.

WEDNESDAY, JULY 5

We go to the burn site today and at the corner of each of the flags, we dig a little square of dirt and sand, in order to measure the depth, in quadrants. I choose to do the recording of all these notes, and therefore spend my time looking for stumps to sit on to write it all down. I am kidded unmercifully for this, but don't mind— at least I am confortable. I must mention again that every time we are at a site, doing work for a little or a long time, someone is always put on "bear watch". The lookout is even given a gun to carry. If a bear appears, the gun would undoubtedly scare him off while we would undoubtedly be speeding in the other direction. We never see a bear while our teammate is defending us! Back to our work... We eat our lunch at the site and continue well into the afternoon. It is a long tiring day. Even sitting on a stump.

One other observance of the day is that there is a "yellow legs", one of our at-home shore birds at the site today, and either he doesn't like our bear-watcher or he doesn't like any of us because he stalks the bear-watcher whenever she comes near him, or yells and screams at the rest of us, as we do our measuring job.

After dinner, we sit and watch the film "Rob Roy" and all of us fall asleep before it is over.

THURSDAY, JULY 6

We work in the lab all morning, making sure the computers have all of the data that we have collected. This is to be part of the briefing for the next team, so they are sure not to repeat any stuff we did. Have lunch, and then out to the plant site area where I redraw some of the grids. We check and recheck all the little plants and shrubs and finish up that particular part of our project.

We come back to the Centre and do some crazy things which we send on to Earthwatch, to the lady who wants us to behave and not be silly. At this point, I'm sure she wouldn't have cared; and we certainly don't either. We gather in one of the rooms to have a small party. One of the team, whose room is next to us, complains we are keeping her awake. We repent— slightly— but keep talking and finally all retire to our beds.

FRIDAY, JULY 7

We are driven to the airport in mid-morning, and get the plane back to Winnepeg. There, we make our different connections to our different destinations. It has been a very special experience in a very special environment and one that I still read about almost every day in my local newspaper. I am sure none of us will ever forget the time we spent at Churchill, Manitoba, Canada.

Front door.

Sign we love to read?

Still melting on Hudson Bay.

The Tundra.

Notice tree branches are on only one side. Too windy.

More tundra.

Checking plantings.

Burnt area. Checking what survived.

July 4th, 2000. Believe!

Icebergs in the Churchill River.

Back from watching Beluga whales.

Remnants from bygone days.

CHAPTER 17

2003: ENGLAND (KETTLEWELL)
ENGLAND'S HIDDEN KINGDOM

INTRODUCTIONS

Once upon a time there was a king named Arthur and he lived in a castle in a place called Camelot. This has been the subject of many books and poems and movies and histories, but nothing matches the imagination of people like me who want to believe it is true. And so when Earthwatch offered a trip/project in the North Yorkshire Dales, of England, in 2003, you might have guessed I would have signed up. The proposal was entitled "In Search of the Ancient British Kingdom of Craven", and we would be using archeological techniques to investigate historical evidence for the existence of this hidden kingdom.

A reappraisal of historical evidence from latter periods has suggested that an independent kingdom may well have emerged in this area when the Roman legions left. Called Rheged, it would have been to the northwest of Craven. This was in the Roman Iron Age and the post Roman era. Already, at one site in the area, there had been found a type of late prehistoric ritual structure ("church"). Preliminary fieldwork had already been done with aerial photography and ground assessment to enhance the interest to archeologists. At nearby Chapel Wood, Roman pottery had been picked up but there are also signs of later occupancy. The Romans left Britain in about 400AD and it is this shadowy period following their withdrawal that is also the time of King Arthur.

Aha! The plot thickens....

THURSDAY/ FRIDAY, JULY 10, 11

I have always heard such charming stories about the Yorkshire Dales that when a trip appears in the yearly catalogue from Earthwatch, I just have to sign up for it. And so on a Thursday night, a friend and I fly from Philadelphia to Manchester, England as the first leg of our journey to Kettlewell. It has been a long night, with delays in Philadelphia, twice, and we are really tired when we get to our city in England. Customs, and then a cab to the railroad station for a train to Leeds. A change here, probably for the good since the city does not look very inviting. As we climb down from the train at the Ilkey station, a cheer goes up from someplace, and we realize we are the last of the Earthwatchers to arrive. Hello, hello, hello. We have lunch at a little pub and pile into the van for our ride out to Kettlewell. Our leader is Roger Martlew, who will soon be known to all of us as Sir Roger.

The villages are charming. Brown stone houses with shingled roofs– steps up and over the stone walls in the meadows, hilly lanes that go up and over little rivers rumbling over stones, and flowers everywhere– in gardens, on front steps, growing out of roof gutters, in window boxes, vases on windowsills, and hanging in baskets from porches and trees.

And then the sheep– also everywhere. They move over the hills and meadows with their lambs trotting behind them. Other ewes stand and call their children to come closer. Some sheep—much the color of the rocks in the meadow– lie near these ancient rocks, and one can hardly tell the difference. Birds sing on fence posts while flowers bend and blow in the gentle cool breeze.

A perfect Eden.

We reach Dale House, which is a little country hotel in the middle of the village of Kettlewell and we are served a delicious supper of chicken, salad and a GREAT lemon pie. We are all exhausted. We are in bed by 9 p.m. and gone for the night.

SATURDAY, JULY 12

Had a good night's sleep and then a good breakfast served downstairs in the dining room. This trip has all the earmarks of being the RIGHT choice.

Sir Roger drives us all around the village and explains how an English village works– at least one this small. A bridge connects the two parts of town and our side is definitely the farm/house and farmland side. Across the bridge are three pubs, a general store, and one gift shop with postcards and a post office. Period! No policemen, no firemen, and no traffic cops, mainly because there are so many sheep being herded to pasture by a farmer with a stick and one or two sheep dogs… no use for traffic cops.

We drive to the site where we are asked to climb the hill while Sir Roger drives up the hill. It is a steep hill and I wished I had been born a mountain goat. Since this is not to be, I offer to do the lab work, instead. Back at the hotel, another volunteer seconds my feeling, so after eating our lunch under a tent that covers the site, in case of inclement weather, we return to Dale House for the afternoon. We are treated to a marvelous lecture by another archeologist on bones. I freak out because I have found my niche. I devour the lecture and am put in charge of bones and whatever else appears in the bags of "finds"—which we are given at the end of each day in the kitchen at Dale House, which becomes our lab.

Archeology is not all about digging. What one digs up needs to be noted in our leader's notebook, brought back to the lab, sorted, washed, dried and put back in the bag to be saved for further study. "It's a dirty job, but someone has to do it!"

So we two volunteers are set. And what fun we have. While the others are up on that hill, digging away, Peggy and I are washing the treasures we have been given, and spend most of our time in the back alley behind Dale House, hosing down all the strange pieces of history. This back alley runs for a whole block, and has the back doors of each house. It develops that all our neighbors are curious about what we are doing. We are "forced" to pretend that we are really an Art Salon. People bring their chairs and their teacups, and Peggy and I hold forth.

We get to know this little village's residents by name and the alley is transformed into a studio setting. Sir Roger and the rest of the Earthwatchers are green with envy at our reports at dinner about what WE find out is going on in the village (we already know what's going on up on the hilltop) and so in 24 hours, we are all family.

SUNDAY, JULY 13

After breakfast, Peggy and I retreat to the kitchen and our bones. One from the group, who should have gone to the site, elbows himself into "our" site and we put him to work and hope he doesn't like what we're doing. (He hates it and never comes back!) So sorry. We lunch and then work until mid-afternoon, when we walk down to the stream across the street, and sit down to put our feet in the water. The three ducks there don't know what or why or who we are, and cruise in and around our feet until they decide that whatever we are—we are boring. At dinner that evening, we sit around and have good talks about the world and we who inhabit it. No solutions.

MONDAY, JULY 14

Everyone is up early because the "bone" lady is coming to examine the bone work in the kitchen. She helps with some identification problems we are having, and then she leaves and the Art Salon continues its work for the rest of the day. In the alley, we talk about flowers as we wash "finds" and the neighbors give us several clues as to why their flowers are so successful. We promise not to tell anyone who is not in the Salon.

Our members increase in number today. We welcome the garbage man, Michael from next door, three-generations of male hikers, and also John Cullin, who is Kettlewell's best known artist. We get several bags of relics all scrubbed and washed and ready to be drawn and identified, and put them back in new plastic bags. After dinner, we have a wonderful lecture by a town person, about the rescue dogs that are often used when someone is lost in the Yorkshire Dales.

TUESDAY, JULY 15

Same old, same old, but we love our work. A cloudy day, so the alley is empty of members and/or visitors. In late afternoon, we stand in the doorway of our house and watch a huge flock of sheep pass. It is interesting to see the shepherd herd them, with a whistle mostly, and the dogs really do nip at the sheep's heels. The sheep ba-ba-ba to each other and take their own time to obey, but they do keep moving. Amazing.

The only out-of-the-ordinary occurrence is after we are all asleep, the three younger members of the group (who have gone pub crawling) find themselves locked out of the house, and throw pebbles at our windows until one of us goes down and lets them in. Don't even think about trying that again!!!

WEDNESDAY, JULY 16

Lucky us– we are brought several bags of dirt to be sifted for the second time. This often happens when so much dirt has been removed from the site that it piles up. The diggers then send it on to the lab for help. "That was really nice of you", we say under our breath. So we sift. And sift. And sift. We are really looking for seeds and pods that might be found, and heaven forbid we should miss even ONE. Actually seeds keep very well over the years, if kept "in situ" (means in its very early environment). Scientists can often tell from seeds just what years, centuries, etc. these seeds were sown. Wow!

After the sifting, Sir Roger drives the two of us to Grassington, a nearby village which has a Police Station. We are impressed because we don't even have one policeman! But someone from the group lost some money in the village and wants to report it. She thinks she left it at one of the pubs. Whoops! Anyway, the police take all the relevant information and are nice to us, and so we ask one of them to become a member of our Art Salon. Sir Roger is a bit shocked by our behavior, but the policeman says he will be over later. He does not show up. Maybe tomorrow?

After lunch, we all go back to our "real" work.

But the best fun of the day is after dinner, when several of us go across the bridge to sit in a pub for the evening. It is Trivia night in which everyone in the pub sits in one room, and writes answers to trivial questions, and the winner gets free beers for the evening. Since we are in England, I glom (?) onto the one member of our Earthwatch team who is a Brit, Sir Roger. Very smart of me (for a change) and of course he and I win. We are accused of conspiracy and so have to share our prize. But what we all love, especially about the evening, is that each of the older men, who come from the bar into our tabled room, brings along his dog. And the dogs lie quietly at their master's feet with a paw or a head resting on his master's boot. Such a picture.

THURSDAY, JULY 17

We continue to sift. I have to describe the size of the sieve. It is about 15 inches of fine chicken meshing attached with nails to a box about 14inches square. The mesh is the bottom of the box. One shakes handfuls of dirt into it and shakes until there is nothing left in the sieve, except of course seeds, pebbles and tiny stuff. All this is then dropped into plastic bags and labeled. We have no trouble doing our jobs, since this obviously doesn't take a rocket scientist to figure out the challenge.

I must mention that, although there are very few noises in this village, during the day, we have to get used to one huge noise, each day, around noon. The Royal Air Force (RAF) Training School is several miles south of us, and the pilots use the dales (not the hills) of Yorkshire to do their daily practice. The first day we hear "them" coming, we think this is IT– we are terrified it is part of an invasion. We find out, as we hurry to the front door, what it is all about, and raise our fists in protest. Not worth it. Each day they harass us again. Soon we learn to ignore them.

After lunch (with the RAF joining us above), a professor comes to our kitchen to help us in our botanical discoveries. Sir Roger has brought her to see us, and he and the 'seed' lady sit and discuss the project. At one point, Peggy and I find a small snail shell in the sieve. We pick it up and hand it to Sir Roger, who jumps out of his chair and shouts "Wow" and grabs the shell. Well, maybe not that bad, but Sir Roger carefully puts it in a little bag and drops it in his pocket. The rest of us wonder if he is going to eat it at dinner.

Since it has been a "grotty" (that means "rainy" in Yorkshire) day, we do not have any alley-work today. But we make a list of the members of our salon: the trash man, Michael (the next-door cook), the hiking men, the artist, Andrew, the Grassington cop, Fred Wolcott (another 83 year old neighbor), and the director of St. Mary's church, which is next to Michael's restaurant. The two of us kitchen workers are the source of local news at each evening meal. But we still have worked hard, and Sir Roger just thinks we're nuts.

FRIDAY, JULY 18

Guess what we are doing today? Still sifting, still washing, still labeling and putting stuff into plastic bags. But the entire group arrives back early and they are carrying many buckets of Querms– late Iron Age farm tools which were used to grind wheat, barley, and corn. The querms are mostly in pieces and we will try to reconstruct them.

Our work is about to change. In the first place, some of these querms are heavy and some of them are large. So we put the buckets in a storage box in the back of the alley and will not be working in the kitchen anymore. The team has begun to clear the site and we are the lucky recipients of their cleansing.

We have lunch, and then we have a good hands-on lecture about all that treasure out in the backyard shed. Not everything in the buckets is big and weighty, thank goodness. We are also discoverers of the usual bones, some teeth, of course, the seeds, some small shards of china, a spindle, and then the early Iron Age querms.

SATURDAY, JULY 19

This is our day OFF. We all pile into Bus #72 bound for Skipton. We travel through gorgeous countryside and fall in love with Yorkshire over and over again. Several from our group get off at Grassington, to go to Bolton Abbey. There are several Abbeys in this area, which makes us think that the foundations of a building found where our team is digging, might, in fact, be that of a spiritual building.

When we get to the town of Skipton, we know we are in a town because there is a Main street and a local market in progress. Fresh produce, clothes on racks, homemade pies and cakes are on tables and in booths. We see the Craven Museum, and then the church where a lady is trying to plant a shrub and obviously needs help. We stop and together get the plant into the ground. Then to the Castle at the end of the road, which is in perfect setting at the end of the town. We buy ice cream cones and other treats, and do some unnecessary shopping, as good visitors should, then get back on our bus and retrace our miles to Kettlewell. Kettlewell looks very nice to us, and we're glad to be back.

After dinner, we go across the street again, to dip our toes in the little stream/river and the ducks pay us no heed at all. Just those boring visitors!

SUNDAY, JULY 20

A few of us go to church today. It is Children's Day at St. Mary's. Our artist friend from the Art Salon is the head usher and the filling-in minister lives two doors from Dale House. This must be what they call "A small world." What did we expect? We talk to them after the service and they are glad we came. So are we. We have lunch together at the Tea Room, the only one in town.

The town is crowded with Sunday hikers, (and their dogs), busses, motorcycles and lots of commotion. It is a lovely day to be outside, here in this English Eden. At dinner, we hear that five of the group had gone overnight to see the great cathedral in York. The rest of us are disappointed that we didn't also go. Maybe another day. We

Chapter 17: England's Hidden Kingdom

order wine for dinner to compensate for our mistake, and then listen to a couple on our team tell about their trip to China. They are good and we all feel better.

MONDAY, JULY 21

Two of us– the Kitchen Kids– finish our work in the Dale House kitchen. We wash everything, and put all our utensils back in the correct drawers. We scrub the counters and the tables we have used and no one would ever know we were there.

At night, Sir Roger gives a lecture at the Racer's Inn. I notice something above the bar and ask the bartender if he realizes that his clock is going backwards. "I was wondering when someone would notice that," he says and does nothing about it. Then I begin to think that maybe I have gone crazy

TUESDAY, JULY 22

Sir Roger brings us more querms from the site, and we scrub them, and mark these pieces out in the alley. We will not mess up our clean kitchen.

After dinner, we go across the village stream to the Trivia Game Night at the pub across the bridge. The team I am on (including Sir Roger) loses, so I stop playing, pet all the dogs that are in the audience, and go back to Dale House. This is called being a sore loser, so just as well I left.

WEDNESDAY, JULY 23

The entire day is in disarray as we try to dismantle the tent over the site, filling in holes that had been dug, collecting the notes that were taken, etc. etc. Stuff is going up and down from the site so fast, one would think we are actually being invaded. Don't remember everything we did, but it was confusing. It also got done.

THURSDAY, JULY 24

This is our final day. We are secretly dreading this day because we have had such a good time. We hope Sir Roger thinks we have done a good job.

We take time to go up to the site (in the van, this time, together) to see the progress that has been made. The site shows the beginning of a prehistoric ritual structure. There is enough evidence of this structure to tentatively say it is a church of some kind or at least a gathering place. There is now a sign of a path leading off to another structure, possibly a house. Based on the finding of a knife from the medieval ages, the spindle from the early Bronze Age, and the shape and condition of the querms, the leaders are sure we have gotten close to the accurate identification.

We get dressed for our "going away" dinner at Dale House, and are given a wonderful meal and lots of wine to go with it. It is great fun and we all make little speeches and tell little stories. Most of them are lies, but that's just part of the fun.

FRIDAY, JULY 25

Sir Roger retraces the miles back to the train station at Illkey and says goodbye to all his volunteers. We all take a deep breath, board the train and start our return trip to our other world we know.

Dale House—our hotel.

The Village.

The stream.

The bridge.

One of the pubs.

The Dales of Yorkshire

We take our orders.

Chapter 17: England's Hidden Kingdom

Another lecture.

I am serious about getting the dirt out.

These are "querms"— old grinding stones

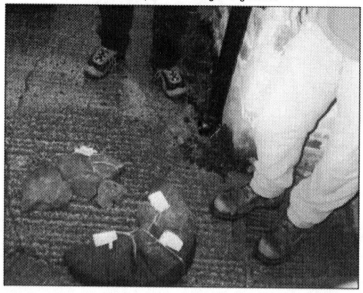

Our last dinner at Dale House

Heavy traffic jam.

CHAPTER 18

2005: UNITED STATES (ELLENSBURG)
CARING FOR CHIMPANZEES

SUNDAY, JUNE 26

As I am flying across the country to the State of Washington, from my home in Philadelphia, I am as excited as I have always been when I set out on an adventure. Somehow I know that this trip is going to be very different than all the others. I also wondered if this was a good choice. But at 30,000 feet in the air, there are no options.

I land in Seattle (Seattle/Tacoma is the airport) and find the bus that I am to take, to the college town of Ellensburg, which is a satellite school of Washington State University. There are no other Earthwatchers on the bus and when the bus driver opens the doors for me to get off in front of the Frontier Bar in Ellensburg, I have a strange feeling I am alone in the midst of nowhere. But within minutes a car arrives, I am greeted by two Earthwatch members, and am whisked off to the campus of the college, and delivered to the dormitory in which the team is to be housed.

The Chimpanzee and Human Communication Institute (CHCI) is at the far end of this large campus. It is away from athletic fields and the football stadium. It sits on grounds surrounded by trees and benches and resembles a park. Today, it houses 4 chimpanzees who were brought here to be studied and from whom the scientists and students hope to learn how best to protect these remarkable animals with a safe environment, a healthy life, and a good and interesting experience.

After dinner that first night, we, Team 3, gather in the living room of our dorm, and begin one of the best two weeks any one us will ever have spent.

The goals here are to ensure the well being of these four chimps and to provide for their individual needs.

MONDAY, JUNE 27

At 7 a.m., we meet in the lobby of our dorm and walk over to the North Village Cafe for breakfast. This is the farthest point from the Institute— at the opposite end of the campus, where we have free meal tickets for the next two weeks. (We will now walk off any pounds we put on, sitting in our classroom). Then we are taken around the entirety of the ground so we can find our way, another day. We arrive at CHCI. We are shown around the facility, including the lab kitchen, the laboratory, the closet where the toys are kept, the offices, and a guided observation of the chimps themselves. As we walk into the observation room, one of the chimps spits water on another, and that starts a huge racket. This translates, we are told, into "Here come the new ones!" Could have fooled me! However, I will continue to be fooled, until I learn more about these hairy creatures. Notice that I use the word hairy; that is because they DO NOT have "fur". They have hair. (Second lesson). At twelve, we all go back to the Cafe for lunch and then traipse back to CHCI for afternoon classes.

We are shown a video of Jane Goodall in Africa and some of the methods she uses when studying her chimps. Fascinating. Then we get our first lesson about our new hairy friends and how to tell them one from another. This is going to be my downfall because basically the four look so much alike.

Washoe is the big momma of the group. She is named for the county in Nevada where she spent her early years. She was born in West Africa, was captured in the wild and later used by the US Air Force. Washoe (Wash-show) is the first non-human to acquire a human language— American Sign Language. She moved in with Roger and Deborah Fouts in 1970 and came with them to Washington University in 1980. She is kind, fair, loyal, and has a sense of humor. She likes magazines,, brushing her teeth, painting, coffee, and tea parties. She loves oatmeal, pumpkin pudding, split pea soup, eggplant, and chewing gum.

If this sounds like a resume, it is.

Tatu is 35 and was born in the US. She joined her friends at CHCI in 1981. She is the most articulate of the chimps and is the smallest of the four. She often signs BLACK which seems to be her favorite color and also refers to anything she particularly likes "as black". She is practical and helpful and also a strict timekeeper. She reminds the interns here when it is time for meals, blanket time, time to go out, etc. She knows Christmas (Sweet Tree) and Thanksgiving (Bird Meat). She loves being outside, rain or shine, and she loves make-up, catalogues, meats, cheeses, and crackers. She is also lactose intolerant so she eats lots of bananas, carrots, and coffee and tea.

She is a sweetheart, to all who know her (that's sounds like a title in her yearbook, but she really is this way).

Then there's <u>Dar</u> who is named for the capitol of Tanzania, and he is 34. He was born in the US ands joined CHCI in 1981. He is a big, easy-going, guy, relaxed, and good-natured and also quite lazy. He enjoys playing outside and is good at Chase, and Tickle(?). He often wears a hat, and he likes shoes and mechanical tools. Banana peels, rice, bread, soda pop, red licorice and ice cream are his menu choices.

The last of the four, who seems to like ME, is <u>Loulis</u>. He is 32 and got his name from Washoe and the letter L that is on the end of his nose. It stands for the word BUG in ASL.

Go figure! He was born in the US and raised with Washoe who adopted him and he learned his first 55 signs from her. He is the first non-human to learn a language from another non-human.

Loulis is the charmer, ranging from sweet to devilish. He is cheerful, playful, and he loves visitors. He is very social, plays games and enjoys mirrors, hats, and naked feet (sounds like a party animal to me!). He eats granola bars and red apples (no green!) and drinks Kool-Aid. And he squeaks when he is excited.

That is the end of our first day. We walk back to the Cafe for dinner and then back to the dorm to sleep.

No problem with sleep. Almost before we shut the room door.

TUESDAY, JUNE 28

Background

Before I go any further, I want you to know that 3x a day, we eat at the North Cafe, where the food is good and we have a nice break from our classes. Some of us squirrel away extra food for lunch, or dinner, so that we don't have to make the trip, back and forth, so often. There are microwaves in our rooms and vending machines for snacks and cold drinks at our dorms. None of us ever starves— just the contrary.

A number of videos are shown to us about conditions, behavior, events and holidays, and other items to do with the chimps' lives here at CHIC. Today we are shown the chimps eating their breakfast in the night enclosure.

Each chimp has his own bedroom, which of course is a cell with a raised slab of concrete as a bed, a trough at the back of the cell which is used when the cell is cleaned (every day!), a door through which food is passed, and a front grill which is strong and protective.

In order to do cleaning chores, the chimps must be moved into spaces out of reach to both them and us. They can sit on railings above us, which they like to do, and watch us work. On my first walk through this area, there is Tatu and Dar, above us. Incidentally, they love to sip on water from bottles while they watch. The next thing I know, I feel a big splotch of water on my t-shirt and look down and then up, and Dar is looking away as if he has no idea what is going on. I learn enough in one day to know to ignore him, and in hindsight, it is really quite funny. (Please aim at my partner, next!)

We will be taught how to gather "data" about chimp behavior including movement and action, but so far, we only will have guided observation in our special room.

We bring our breakfast to the classroom and while we eat, we watch the chimps eating their breakfast, via the remote video. Strangely enough it is not that different, since they are using spoons and bowls, and we are using forks and knives. However, they often use their fingers, and we're not supposed to do that. And, I do not like oatmeal with onions in it, and they probably would not like my Danish.

We have classes from 9 a.m. to 12 p.m. and then break for lunch.

I want to tell you about the geography of the Institute. There is a lobby inside the front door, which has a gift shop, a bulletin board, and a special show board, which changes from time to time... artwork, photographs, personnel, etc. There is a hall to your right with offices and directly in front of you is the classroom. To the left of the classroom is a passage that leads into the observation room, with tiers of benches. It looks into two playrooms, each 2000 square feet, and connected at the back. To the farther left is the door to the outdoor area, which is 5000 square feet of grass, shrubs, trees, and concrete panels and platforms (3 stories high) and around all this, is a ledge that runs around the whole area. There are tall, large Plexiglas windows from ground to ceiling. The inside of the "outdoor room" is filled with fire hoses and truck tires, hanging here and there, cargo nets hang like hammocks, swings of half tires, fencing, toilets, a cave, and cement climbing structures. What more could a kid want?

And the chimps love it. They toot and run around, and play games. On the top ledge, at the back of the area, is where Washoe stands each morning, waiting for Prof. and Mrs. Fouts to arrive in their car, park in the parking lot, walk into the Institute, and then leaps down and runs to the little balcony where the Fouts will stop each morning and say hello to their favorite four animals.

At the back of the indoor playrooms are the sleeping and eating cages, where the chimps spend time doing one or the other. From their cages, they can see us at work in the kitchen preparing their meal, and they hoot and holler, in anticipation. At night they are calmed down with a popsicle and their own blanket, which they hold around themselves and fall asleep.

Now back to our daily schedule.

We have class until 5 p.m., leave for dinner at the Cafe, drift back to the dorm and do chores and go to bed.

WEDNESDAY, JUNE 29

I am on duty to clean cages at 9 a.m., so go to the Cafe early. Five of us work together which means we each have a cage and then some. I have described what the cells look like, so with borrowed boots and a hose, turned on, we go through the first door, and LOCK it, pick up a pail, broom, mop, and shovel, and through the 2nd door, and LOCK it, and get to work. The chimps have been sent above at a safe distance and love to watch us work. Sometimes they spit at us. Thanks, but been there, done that! The cell is scrubbed down from top to bottom, and everything in the cell goes swishing down the trough, or the blankets and toys get thrown in a container, to be washed in a machine. We do not look up at them or antagonize them, or even admit we know they are there.

When we are done, we leave the place immaculate, remove ourselves, all tools and pails, go through the first door and LOCK it (incidentally, we have LOCKED all the cell doors also and each one of us checks each other) leave our boots in the room and go through the second door and LOCK it. After two weeks of this, we will qualify to be good prison guards!

After lunch we return to the classroom, and get to go to the observation room to sit and observe. As we approach, we can see Washoe sitting close to a grate in the wall and on the other side of the grate sits a graduate student, turning the pages of a catalogue of flowers. When she turns the page too slowly, Washoe taps her finger on the glass and says something unprintable. But reader nods, and speeds up.

THURSDAY, JUNE 30

Today, it's breakfast, then CHIC, and a new group of cell cleaners. The rest of us go to class and then out to the observation room. We are being taught how to tell the chimps apart. Tatu is the smallest, but when she is standing alone, she doesn't look that small! Uh, oh, this is not going to be easy.

Washoe— has whitish hair, a heavy brow ridge...round ears, rounded nostrils.

Tatu— has a pointy nose, pointed ears... quite bald behind the brow ridge, slightly more rounded body, i.e. female, thinner face.

Dar— light brown hair on his back, floppy ears, which bend, large brow, mottled face, eyes set way back, long arms, pale face.

Loulis— short and stout, muscular, ridge over brow is emphasized, tennis-ball-in-his-mouth look, round ears, callouses on back of hands, pale face, shorter arms.

Gee! No trouble at all, except it would be easier if they each wear a different colored hair that day, or at least a bow in their hair, or a tie around their neck. Wishful thinking.

FRIDAY, JULY 1

Breakfast and then classes with some new info. Let's look at our hands and compare with a chimp. Hold your right hand out in front of you. Thumb automatically veers off to the right. Try it with a chimp— and his thumb will line up alongside of his other fingers. And yet, we have such close DNA (98.76%) that you would think our fingers would match.

When we go to observe the chimps, we must remove hats/hoods, and no chewing gum or candy. No cameras allowed and no cell phones.

Certain signs you may use when observing are: hello, sorry, friend, hugs (love), thank you, dirty, and goodbye.

Today seems to be made especially for me. I have three jobs. In the morning I must help clean the cages. I've already explained what that involves, so won't go through it again. At least I can wear a clean t-shirt and not worry about any spit from above. After lunch I am on duty to prepare dinner for the little guys (misnomer— big guys). The kitchen has a huge refrigerator with all the "makings" of meals. Not for us, thank goodness. And the menus have been posted for us to follow. So it is just a matter of chopping and slicing and peeling and boiling, and then every thing goes into a huge pot and into the huge refrigerator, and the "servers" for that night only have to spoon out and serve those four gaping mouths that appear through the kitchen windows.

The next job is really fun and creative. It is called enrichment, and simply means going into the toy closet, selecting a number of toys with which to entertain the chimps the next day, and filling up two wicker laundry baskets with all of it. Enrichment is a fancy term for keeping the guys occupied in the playrooms. This becomes a real show, because without any coaxing, the four begin to run around in hats, dressers, shawls, furry slippers, and whatever else they think is fashionable. Every week or so, a play pool is put in one room for them to contemplate. Tatu hates water, so she sits aside, and thinks other thoughts. Dar would like to stretch out in the pool but can't fit. So he lies sidewise and dips his hands and feet in. The others wade in and out, and drink, and taste. Enrichments include some of the following: shoes, gloves, hats, crayons with lots of colored paper, books, shredded paper for?, pictures, masks, buckets, brushes, shovels, stuffed animals, and balls.

Enough for one day!

SATURDAY, JULY 2

A Moment to Digress

Regular scenario except that at 11:30 am, my job is to go to the kitchen and make banana bread for the chimps. I, of course, shall sample this as I go, to make sure it is tasty. Ahem. Before I go into the wide array of food that is given to the chimps, I must remind you that the chimps are not "given" food, no, they are "served". I almost was exiled when I used the wrong verb!

They are fed three meals a day:

Breakfast: vitamins, smoothies, and fruit.

Lunch: cooked soup, crackers, and vegetables.

Dinner: (more starch) rice, pasta, potatoes, cereal- oatmeal or farina.

Chimps eat from bowls with spoons.

This is a funny vignette that I heard one day as I was passing through the kitchen. One of the interns, named Jason, was busy chopping up onions for Tatru.

Tatu- signs: Gimme!

Jason- "Wait.

Tatu- "Hurry, Gimme food".

Jason- "What kind of food?"

Tatu- "Corn".

Jason- "We don't have corn; we only have onions".

Tatu- "Onions". (Crooks finger toward Jason and rubs her left eye).

Jason- "I'll go get onions".

Tatu- "Hurry, gimme food".

This was all done by signing. I went on my way shaking my head in disbelief.

Today is our day off. We sleep later, and don't have to rush. We do chores and go into the village to buy necessities and then have an early lunch. Our excursion today starts with swimming in the water at Peter's Pond. This is an option, which only a few choose because the water is FREEZING cold. When you look around at the scenery— tall pine trees on beautiful mountains, it seems logical that the water in this state would not be like swimming in Bermuda. We can all sun and play around the park and catch minnows and skim stones. Finally, we pack up and move on in our van to Lion's Rock, which sits on top of the mountains that we have only seen from below. It is the high point, with a large picnic area and we unload the car, start a campfire, and hike around the territory. This is a lovely state, and we can't get over the thick forests. There is a cabin nearby with several horses that we are told roam the forest but love to see humans arrive. We are lent some fruits to feed these gorgeous creatures and then they stamp and snort and go their way through the trees. If a unicorn had walked out of that forest, I wouldn't have been surprised.

We have a nice cook-out, and just sort of loll around, and then twilight begins to sneak in and we pack up and drive back to CHIC. We all stop to see that the chimps are safe and sound, and then move on to the dorm and a nice night's sleep.

SUNDAY, JULY 3

Even though it is Sunday, there is no rest. Again, I am on duty as one of the cell maids, so with boots on my feet, and shovels and hoses in hand, I perform the ritual of the hired help. In the PM. we begin our lectures on collecting "data". This will be our work for the rest of our week, and of our stay here at the Institute.

We are to use clipboards and make charts of the locomotive action of the chimps, particularly in their outdoor area. This locomotion behavior of each chimp will be recorded at strict intervals, entered on our charts, and identified by a series of categories describing their moves. For example: bp = back up (the chimp moves backward), br-bipedal run = chimp runs on his feet, bw = bipedal walk (chimp walks on his feet), qr = quadrupedal run (chimp runs on both knuckles and feet), sp = spin (Loulis does this a lot with one foot planted firmly on the ground). How about that for homework! There are 26 such abbreviations for whatever locomotion moves we see and each one has to be charted. There is little conversation during dinner or after, since we are terrified of this daunting new development. I think that maybe I could catch an early bus back to Seattle or apply for a permanent job as a cell-cleaner. We do not sleep well. We are too apprehensive.

MONDAY, JULY 4

At least I don't have to clean cages today. Instead, right after our morning arrival at CHIC, all of us go to the outdoor space. We are still inside a glass partition and the four chimps are cavorting around in their outdoor playroom. Each of us is assigned one chimp and we are to chart his/her locomotive behavior for 15 minutes. This may sound simple, but it is like trying to keep an eye on one of your children, who is racing around the beach, running into the water, racing back to you the next minute— - you get the picture; it's called perpetual motion. Any way, I am given Tatu as my subject. By the time our fifteen minutes is up, I am cross-eyed and exhausted. My chart looks totally useless and I struggle for some time interpreting my own symbols and putting then in the correct columns, etc. I consider that I may lose my mind in the course of this assignment; but I am driven by self-preservation to continue. Strangely enough, after several more sessions, collecting data, I begin to get the hang of it, and eventually I settle down and realize I CAN do it. After lunch, we continue our eye-gymnastics, and at 3 p.m., I am excused to go and prepare the dinners for the chimps. A kitchen never looked more appealing to me before. I boil the oatmeal and season it with the onions and herbs, and make some rice, and put out the bowls/spoons/fruit, etc. and leave the room. (No napkins provided) The interns serve the food since this is another time when one has to go through locked doors, before and after, and I think our basic training is not sufficient to entitle us to do all this, carrying food, etc. That's okay with us.

We all gather in the toy closet to select tomorrow's playthings, and then our dinner is brought over to our dorm for us. I forget what was going on at the Cafe, but we are not included. No problem. After a day's work, we, truthfully, could eat anywhere.

TUESDAY, JULY 5

The usual calendar of behavior for us.

I am on call for cleaning cages this morning, but I have become so expert at this chore that I whiz through without even thinking. I did think I heard a sound from up in the rafters, once, which sounded like a laugh, and the another time I thought someone was applauding us, but ignored my tendency to look up at (them?) and kept on working.

Then in the afternoon, after doing some more data collecting, we all went to the toy closet and filled up the wicker baskets again. Some of the grad students or interns collect the previous days toys, separate some back on their rightful shelves, or throw some in the washing machine, or throw some of the stuff away. (Like shredded papers and torn magazines.) We volunteers are spared that duty.

WEDNESDAY, JULY 6

Repeat performances for all, except I don't have to clean cages.

THURSDAY, JULY 7

Aha! Good things keep happening. I jest! Today I am back on "cleaning detail". But that is okay because we have an early lunch scheduled at the Cafe so we can pick up tidbits to squirrel away for tomorrow. We will NOT be collecting data tomorrow because it will be our last day at CHIC and we will hear the truth and consequences about what is currently being done, and what is planned for the future for these four wonderful creatures which we have come to love, honor and respect.

So in the afternoon I again prepare the dinner for the chimps, and really would like to give them pizza and hamburgers, and potato chips, and milk shakes, and Snicker Bars, but the menu says NO to all my good (bad?) intentions. Apparently someone else knows better than I do— or there would be sick animals and I would be in disgrace.

Instead we have a Potluck dinner out on the front lawn of CHIC and each of us brings a side dish to complete the meal. That is sort of tricky because we each want to bring our recipe from home. We are all limited because we have no place to cook— only microwave— but we come up with a variety of specialties (albeit occasionally on the strange side?) but plates and bowls are cleared, and we all go back indoors for brownies and ice cream. We don't invite the four other members of the "household" but they are happy elsewhere. They probably have nice treats at bedtime.

FRIDAY, JULY 8

Usual breakfast.

We have a very good morning in our classroom and learn about the myriad of efforts to improve the psychological well being of chimpanzees in captivity. First we are elated, and then we are frantic with worry, and we go from bad to better, and actually "all over the place". It is both a rewarding and a devastating report. (More in my own summary on the next page). At 2:30 pm, there is a little ceremony for us volunteers. Everyone is feted in one word or another, and my heart shrinks when my turn comes. But they are kind, and although it has taken me more time than any of the others to learn to tell the chimps apart, successfully, I did finally GET it, and graduated. Awful thing is that I will probably NEVER forget that test and will probably wake up frantically from sleep, now and then, wondering if I got the characteristics right or wrong. However...

Then we are allowed to go into the observation room with our cameras and take pictures of the four stars. And we all buy copies of the book "Next of Kin" which are autographed by the authors— the Fouts, here at CHIC.

There are many sniffles, and blinking back of tears when we leave our friends (both human and almost-human). That afternoon, there is a box of Kleenex for us at the door. We take it and walk back to our dorm.

SATURDAY, JULY 9

Our breakfast has been packed for us to eat on our train/bus/shuttle after we turn in our keys, early in the day. The Earthwatcher's schedules differ from one to the next, and by noon, we are on our separate routes home.

A rare and magical experience. It could have only happened with Earthwatch's bright opportunity.

CLOSING COMMENTS:

In closing, this is what I want to remember about the Chimpanzees. Maybe you would like to remember this also.

Chimps have a 6-year dependency on their mothers and yet many of them were snatched from their mother's back, while still in the wild, and taken to the US by the Air Force to be used/trained by NASA for flights into space before using humans.

Chimps have similar emotional ands cognitive reactions, as we do... i.e. visual acuity, sensitivity to light colors in the spectrum, differences in size, perception of movement, hearing ability, feeling for hot and cold, and they also get high on alcohol.

They are very territorial.

They make their own tools... i.e. they use a stone on a rock to crack seeds and nuts.

When they are in the wild and decide to go hunting for food they a) collaborate with each other b) form a group c) appoint a driver, a chaser, several blockers and an ambusher. (Anyone for football?)

Chimps come from the West Coast of Africa, near Jane Goodall's study in Tanzania.

They acquire knowledge from learning— it is not innate.

They can live 40-50 years of age in the wild; less in captivity

Tatu has been crippled with rickets from being in a cramped cage at a Bio-Medical facility and has trouble going up and down steps.

In her first snowfall, Tatu had trouble getting the snow off her hands and feet and tried by twirling around in a cargo net!

There are Chimposiums given at CHIC for the public. The workshop lasts one hour.

American Sign Language—the chimps currently can sign 150-300 words. They cannot produce vowels, due to a certain lack of mobility of their tongue. Their throats and larynxes are formed differently than ours, which prevents the chimps from vocalizing. (Supra laryngeal pharyngareal) Go look it up! In ASL there are signs for various dialects and accents, and the chimps know some of these. They also create some of their own sign language. (Don't ask!)

In the world of entertainment, circuses, etc. chimps are often trained with a pipe that has been wrapped in newspaper. They are struck for doing something wrong. No wonder they are terrified when they see a newspapel. And they grin when they are frightened. (I wonder how they would look if they read one of OUR newspapers? Probably the same!)

End of the extras about our students at CICC. Just know that there are about 3000 chimps in captivity in the USA—still, 1400 in Bio-Medical institutions, 1000 in private homes and entertainments, 600 minimum and growing in zoos and sanctuaries.

We can all help these animals by educating ourselves and others; by avoiding African woods such as teak and mahogany (cutting down the trees pushes these animals out of their habitat) and avoiding media which exploits primates.

And for your own safety, never pat a chimp on the head; it's worse than putting your hand in a lion's mouth.

Portrait of Tatu.

The left-side of the Chimpanzee and Human Communication Institute (CHCI)

The right-side of CHCI.

Classroom attendance.

This is the way we wash the cages.

Chimp's play area (outside).

Chimp's play area outside but still inside.

Good-bye party.

The chimps' staff.

Layout of CHCI.

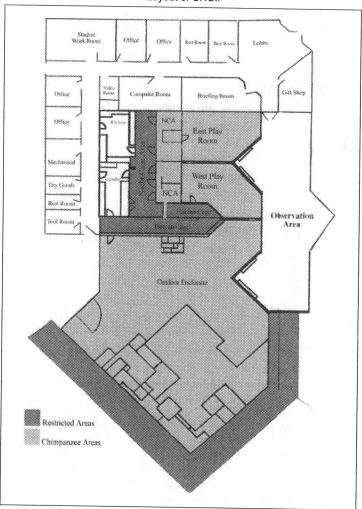

Student Work Room · Office · Office · Rest Room · Rest Room · Lobby

Office · Video Room · Computer Room · Briefing Room · Gift Shop

Office · Mechanical · Dry Goods · Rest Room · Tool Room

NCA · East Play Room

West Play Room

NCA · Human Unit

Night House Unit

Outdoor Enclosure

Observation Area

Restricted Areas
Chimpanzee Areas